RUSSIA
After Communism

Anders Åslund and
Martha Brill Olcott,
Editors

Carnegie Endowment for International Peace
Washington, D.C.

© 1999 by the
Carnegie Endowment for International Peace
1779 Massachusetts Avenue, N.W.
Washington, D.C. 20036
Tel. (202) 483-7600
Fax. (202) 483-1840

Russia After Communism
ISBN 0-87003-151-1 (paper) $16.95

To order, contact Carnegie's distributor:
The Brookings Institution Press
Department 029, Washington, D.C. 20042-0029, USA
Tel: 1-800-275-1447 or 202-797-6258
Fax: 202-797-6004, E-mail: bibooks@brook.edu
Web: www.ceip.org

Library of Congress Cataloging-in-Publication Data
Russia after communism / Anders Åslund, editor, Martha Brill Olcott,
    editor.
        p.   cm.
    ISBN 0-87003-151-1
    1. Russia (Federation)—History—1991- . 2. Post-communism—Russia
(Federation).   I. Åslund, Anders, 1952-   .   II. Olcott, Martha Brill, 1949-   .
DK510-76.R86   1999   97-24227
947.-896—dc21   CIP

Cover design: Laurie Rosenthal
Printing: Automated Graphic Systems, Inc.

Contents

iii

Foreword

Since the collapse of the Soviet Union in 1991, Russia has undergone a transformation as complex and wrenching as the transition *to* communism in the early decades of this century. That the current transition takes place without major loss of life or destruction of property (with the exception of the war in Chechnya) in no way diminishes the magnitude of the undertaking or the uncertainty of its course.

The building of post-Soviet Russia is now seven years along—not a long time in comparison with the seventy-five years of communism that preceded it, but long enough for scholars to reflect on the early record of successes, failures, false starts, and new beginnings. The essays in this book treat subjects as diverse as the creation of new political, civil, and economic institutions; the conduct of elections; the search for a national identity; and the development of foreign relations with more than a dozen countries that did not even exist as independent states until December 1991. In each of these areas, the most difficult task was not sweeping away communist ideology, which was already discredited before the fall of the Soviet Union, but undoing the results of decades of bad practices and perverse incentives and replacing these with positive counterparts.

It goes without saying that Russia's future is of more than academic interest. Russian statesmen of all political persuasions believe that their country should play a major role in world affairs. Despite its current economic weakness and political uncertainty, Russia retains the potential to do much to advance—or to frustrate—the policies of the United States and its European allies. Increased stability and prosperity in Russia would make an immense difference in the lives of millions of Russian citizens, but the indirect benefits of these good things would be felt worldwide. Likewise, chaos and violence, virulent nationalism, border wars, or economic collapse in Russia would disrupt much more than Russia itself.

The history of Russia after communism provides important and humbling lessons for those who study or work in such fields as democracy building and economic development. The West has provided extensive assistance to Russia, but the essays in this book reveal where it could have done more—or have done what it did more skillfully—to advance the reforms and to solidify their achievements.

Anders Åslund and Martha Olcott, the editors of *Russia After Communism*, are both senior associates at the Carnegie Endowment for International Peace. They were fortunate to recruit a team of contributors who combined scholarly expertise with practical experience as government ministers and advisors to government officials and political party leaders. By fortunate coincidence, all nine authors are currently affiliated with the Carnegie Endowment and are engaged in new research on Russia and its neighbors, including additional collaborative projects involving colleagues in the Endowment's Washington and Moscow offices.

Jessica T. Mathews
President

April 1999
Washington, D.C.

Acknowledgments

This volume grew out of a workshop held at the Carnegie Endowment for International Peace in Washington in November 1996, which was attended by all the authors and by Stephen Sestanovich (then vice president of Carnegie's Russian and Eurasian Program) and Scott Bruckner (then director of the Carnegie Moscow Center), as well as by Charles Fairbanks, Clifford Gaddy, Michael Mandelbaum, Joseph Pelzman, Frederick Starr, and Angela Stent. The authors of this volume benefited from the criticism of all the workshop participants and are grateful for the detailed comments which they provided.

We also wish to acknowledge the assistance of our junior fellows. This volume would not have been possible without the time and efforts of Marcus Fellman, Rachel Lebenson, Dennis Maslov, Maria Popova, and Judith Smelser. We also benefited from the comments and criticisms of our Carnegie colleagues Aleksei Malashenko and Galina Vitkovskaya. Finally, we are indebted to the following administrators and researchers of the Carnegie Russian and Eurasian Program: Arnold Horelick, vice president; David Kramer, associate director; Natalia Udalova, project associate; Elisabeth Reisch, research assistant; and, of course, Alan Rousso, director of the Carnegie Moscow Center.

Chronology of Key Events, 1985–1998

March 11, 1985	Mikhail Gorbachev becomes general secretary of the Communist Party of the Soviet Union.
December 1, 1988	USSR Supreme Soviet approves law providing for contested elections.
March 1989	Elections held in the USSR for a new legislature, the Congress of People's Deputies.
February–September 1990	All Soviet republics hold competitive elections for republican Supreme Soviets.
March 11, 1990	Lithuanian Supreme Soviet declares Lithuania's independence.
March 14, 1990	Gorbachev elected USSR president by the Congress of People's Deputies.
March 30, 1990	Estonian Parliament announces the beginning of a transition to independence.
May 1990	Latvia's Supreme Soviet votes to restore Latvia's independence.
May 29, 1990	Boris Yeltsin elected chairman of Russia's Supreme Soviet.
August 1990	Stanislav Shatalin's group of economists develops a 500-day plan for economic reform.
March 17, 1991	All-union referendum held on preserving the USSR.
June 12, 1991	Boris Yeltsin elected president of Russia with 57.3 percent of the vote.
August 19–21, 1991	Unsuccessful coup attempt against Gorbachev.
August–September 1991	Most Soviet republics declare independence.
September 6, 1991	USSR recognizes the independence of the Baltic states.

October 28, 1991	Yeltsin delivers programmatic speech on economic reform.
November 6–8, 1991	Yeltsin assumes the post of prime minister in addition to his presidential post and forms an economic reform government with deputy prime ministers Gennady Burbulis, Yegor Gaidar, and Aleksandr Shokhin.
December 1, 1991	90 percent of Ukrainians vote for independence in a referendum.
December 7–8, 1991	At a meeting in Belovezhskaya Pushcha (Belarus), the leaders of Russia, Ukraine, and Belarus decide to end the Soviet Union and to create the Commonwealth of Independent States (CIS).
December 21, 1991	The CIS is expanded to eleven countries at a meeting in Alma-Ata.
December 25–26, 1991	Gorbachev resigns as president of the USSR. The Soviet flag on the Kremlin is replaced with the Russian tricolor. Russia assumes the Soviet seat in the United Nations.
January 2, 1992	Prices are liberalized on most products.
March 31, 1992	Russian federal treaty is signed by all republics except Tatarstan and Chechnya.
May 15, 1992	Russia, Kazakhstan, Kyrgyzstan, Uzbekistan, Moldova, and Armenia sign a collective security treaty in Tashkent.
May–June 1992	Three former enterprise managers, including Victor Chernomyrdin, become deputy prime ministers.

June 1, 1992	Russia joins the International Monetary Fund (IMF).
June 11, 1992	Supreme Soviet adopts a privatization program for 1992.
June 15, 1992	Yeltsin appoints Yegor Gaidar acting prime minister.
July 1992	Russia signs a standby agreement with the IMF, which fails immediately.
December 1992	Voucher privatization of mid-sized and large enterprises begins.
December 12–14, 1992	Viktor Chernomyrdin replaces Yegor Gaidar as prime minister.
March 28, 1993	Congress of People's Deputies attempts and fails to impeach Yeltsin.
April 25, 1993	Yeltsin and his government's economic reform policies receive a vote of confidence in a national referendum.
May 1993	Russia and the IMF sign an agreement on a Systemic Transformation Facility.
July 24, 1993	Old Soviet ruble banknotes are declared void by the Russian Central Bank.
September 21, 1993	Yeltsin dissolves Congress of People's Deputies and the Supreme Soviet.
October 3–4, 1993	Armed uprising in Moscow; military units storm the Russian parliament.
December 12, 1993	New Russian constitution is adopted in a referendum. Elections to the State Duma are held. Party of nationalist leader Vladimir Zhirinovsky wins biggest share of the vote.

January 5, 1994	Russia and Belarus sign an agreement on monetary union.
January 1994	Resignations of Yegor Gaidar, first deputy prime minister, and Boris Fedorov, finance minister.
April 20, 1994	Russia and the IMF renew their Systemic Transformation Facility agreement.
October 11, 1994	"Black Tuesday"—the collapse of the exchange rate of the ruble.
November 5, 1994	Anatoly Chubais appointed first deputy prime minister in charge of economic affairs.
December 12, 1994	Russia moves troops into break-away republic of Chechnya.
April 11, 1995	Russia and the IMF conclude a standby agreement for a $6.8 billion loan.
October–December 1995	Loans-for-shares privatization program.
December 16, 1995	Duma elections held. Communists win largest share of the vote (22.3 percent).
January 1996	Yeltsin removes Chubais from all his government positions.
March 26, 1996	Russia and the IMF conclude a three-year Extended Fund Facility (EFF) agreement for a $10.1 billion loan.
April 2, 1996	Russia, Kyrgyzstan, Kazakhstan, and Belarus sign a treaty on deeper integration and form the Community of Sovereign States.
April 26, 1996	China, Russia, Kazakhstan, and Kyrgyzstan sign border delimitation agreement.

June 16, 1996	Yeltsin narrowly defeats Communist Party candidate Gennady Zyuganov in the first round of presidential elections.
June 20, 1996	Yeltsin dismisses Oleg Soskovets, first deputy prime minister, and Aleksandr Korzhakov, head of the president's security service.
July 3, 1996	Yeltsin wins landslide victory in presidential runoff election.
July 1996	Chubais appointed presidential chief of staff. Chernomyrdin reconfirmed as prime minister. Alexander Lebed named secretary of the Security Council.
September 25, 1996	Russia and Chechnya sign an armistice brokered by Lebed.
October 17, 1996	Lebed dismissed as secretary of the Security Council.
October 31, 1996	Boris Berezovsky appointed deputy secretary of the Security Council.
November 5, 1996	Yeltsin undergoes heart bypass surgery.
Late 1996–early 1997	Fifty-two gubernatorial elections are held in Russia.
March 1997	Yeltsin reshuffles government, appoints Chubais and Boris Nemtsov (governor of Nizhny Novgorod) as the only two first deputy prime ministers.
April 2, 1997	Russia and Belarus sign Treaty on Union, which provides for common citizenship, common currency, and joint armed forces.
May 27, 1997	NATO–Russia Founding Act signed in Paris.

May 28, 1997	Russia and Ukraine sign an agreement on the status of the Black Sea fleet.
End of July 1997	25 percent of Russian telecommunications giant Svyazinvest sold in an open auction. The deal triggers the so-called Bankers War.
November 4, 1997	Boris Berezovsky loses his post at the Security Council.
Mid-November 1997	Three members of the Chubais team are dismissed. Chubais remains deputy prime minister but loses his post as a finance minister.
March 23, 1998	Yeltsin dismisses the Chernomyrdin government and appoints Sergei Kiriyenko as new prime minister. Deputy prime ministers Anatoly Chubais and Anatoly Kulikov are fired.
July 13, 1998	Russia secures a $22 billion loan from the IMF, the World Bank, and Japan.
August 17, 1999	Russia devalues the ruble, defaults on its domestic treasury bills (GKOs), and imposes a ninety-day moratorium on international debt service.
August 23, 1998	Yeltsin fires the Kiriyenko government and nominates Chernomyrdin as prime minister.
August 31, 1998	Duma overwhelmingly rejects Chernomyrdin's candidacy for the first time.
September 7, 1998	Duma overwhelmingly rejects Chernomyrdin's candidacy for the second time; Yeltsin then withdraws nomination.
September 11, 1998	Duma confirms Yevgeny Primakov as prime minister.

INTRODUCTION |

Anders Åslund and Martha Brill Olcott

Over the past decade Moscow has gone from being one of the world's drabbest capital cities to among the world's most dynamic ones. Bare-shelved state-owned stores have been replaced by glittering malls and boutiques filled with merchandise from all over the world. Placards and political slogans have all come down from billboards and other public spaces, their places taken by brightly-colored advertisements. Flights in and out of Moscow now are filled with Russian tourists rather than Westerners. New buildings have gone up throughout the city, and trash dumps have been heaped with the discarded desiderata of Russia's Soviet past.

Many of these changes, though, have come at high human cost. The same economic changes that produced the new rich have created a vast new underclass. Beggars and homeless persons are frequent sights in the cities, and many come from the old Soviet white-collar class. Hundreds of thousands of refugees now live in Russia, some from Chechnya and others fleeing wars in neighboring states. Street crime, kidnapping, murder, and even terrorism—once virtually unheard of—are now features of Russian life. The nature of the "new" Russia is a subject of debate for all who lived in or near Russia, or are otherwise concerned with it. Even now, nearly eight years later, there is little agreement on what the breakup of the USSR means for the future of Russia or the West.

In retrospect, the collapse of the Soviet Union may be the most profound event of the last half of the twentieth century. A country occupying one-sixth of the earth's surface dissolved into fifteen new states virtually overnight. The demise of the USSR also brought with it the discrediting of the communist system—its political institutions, economic system, and social values. Few observers were prepared for the speed with which this occurred, or for the enormity of the changes that it would create.

This book looks at developments in Russia, the largest, most populated, and most strategically important of these countries. Russia is simultaneously a new and a very old state. Its current borders are new ones, but this country is also heir to both the USSR and the Russian empire. This has complicated the task of building a new state and creating a new national identity, as the Russians try to sustain old traditions and acquire new values.

Russia's leaders and citizens have found it difficult to gain their bearings in this rapidly changing new era. The country's political institutions have been transformed. Russia is a partly-formed democracy; its citizens go to the polls regularly to elect their president, national legislators, governors, and local legislators. Whether there is enough elite or mass support for these institutions to sustain them over time is less certain: the first real test of their durability will only come when Boris Yeltsin passes from the political scene.

The old Soviet command economy has been shattered, but the transition to a market economy has been a rough and incomplete one. Privatization is seemingly irreversible, but as long as the rudimentary market economy that has been formed remains dysfunctional, the nature and timetable of Russia's economic recovery remain unclear.

The incomplete nature of Russia's political and economic transformation has complicated the problem of creating political loyalty, keeping alive a national political debate over just whom the Russian political state is intended to serve. The current climate works to the advantage of those who hold extreme political views, be they nationalists or communists. Some would like to see Russia break up or decentralize, while others are nostalgic for an imperial past. Yet increasingly people are beginning to realize that neither by consent nor by force can Russia absorb other Soviet successor states and recreate the Soviet Union. The Russian Empire cannot be resuscitated, but Russia will continue to pressure neighboring former Soviet republics more than they would like.

Our purpose in writing this book is to point out the factors that are shaping the political and economic systems that are emerging in Russia. We have tried to bring out key aspects of domestic politics, nation building, economics, and policy toward the neighborhood of the new Russia, to give the reader a sense of the possible shape of future developments.

Ours is a joint effort of Americans and Russians who have worked closely with each other for years. All of the authors have had lengthy associations with the Carnegie Moscow Center, which, since its opening in 1993, has provided a forum where scholars and experts on Russia and the other new countries of the post-Soviet space exchange views and shape their understandings of what has or should happen to these newly formed or re-formed nations. Each essay is written jointly by a Westerner and a Russian and reflects a set of recurrent themes from our seminars in Moscow. Russian and Western scholars now tend to work with the same intellectual paradigms, but their perspectives often vary. The authors of these essays have tried to find common ground—to explain what assumptions they shared and what questions were still controversial. All the authors of the volume have, to varying degrees, been participants in the creation of the new Russia—as ministers, senior government advisors, consultants to political parties and groups, scholarly observers, or commentators on the Russian post-Soviet scene.

WHAT WE FOUND

Lilia Shevtsova and Martha Brill Olcott focus on political institution building in their chapter, "Russia Transformed." They reach the somewhat gloomy conclusion that, despite political and economic liberalization and privatization, Russia has experienced no significant growth in the sector outside of government control. In part, this has been the result of a deliberate attempt by those in power to maintain as much control of society as possible. Shevtsova and Olcott find this disturbing on two counts. First, the near symbiosis between government and business has led to the failure of most elite members to distinguish between the national interest and their own. Second, the more the government interferes, the weaker it grows—as demonstrated by its inability to control crime, collect revenues, maintain public order, mount an effective military, and ensure that its authority is respected in the periphery. Although they consider these tendencies a distinct threat to the future of democracy in Russia, the authors acknowledge that these developments have partly democratic roots, insofar as they are efforts by the elite to respond to the wishes of the electorate, which favors stability after a period of extreme volatility. To date both the elite and the population have been self-restraining. The people have been battered by economic losses, deteriorating public order, reduced international prestige of their state, and fear of interethnic conflict. Nonetheless, they appear to prefer the present system, whatever its faults, to uncertainty.

In their chapter, "The Changing Function of Elections in Russian Politics," Michael McFaul and Nikolai Petrov provide a systematic analysis of the six major national elections Russia held from 1989 to 1996. They compare the Russian path with a typical process of democratization, and they reject the nostrum that there is something unique, or uniquely self-destructive, about Russian behavior. Russia has become a state in which elections are common and in which voter participation is quite high. A disturbing anomaly, however, is that these elections have brought little replacement of the power elite from the Soviet era, neither at the federal nor at the regional levels. Frequent elections have not stimulated the growth of a multi-party system, as is typical in other states making the transition to democracy. Perhaps most serious is that the elections have not become more transparent over time. Indeed, elections in Russia were in some ways less free and fair in 1996 than they were in 1991. At the same time, McFaul and Petrov note a growing tendency among the communist-era elite to take elections seriously. There are many positive tendencies: the election laws have become firmer and better enforced; the nomination and ballot-counting procedures have become simpler; and the number of contestants per seat is rising. As a result, the authors cautiously conclude that a transformation of the political system has indeed taken place.

In "From Ethnos to Demos: The Quest for Russia's Identity," Valery Tishkov and Martha Brill Olcott discuss how the development of civic nationalism in Russia is complicated by lingering effects of the Soviet practice of basing political rights not on individuals but on ethnic groups. In the USSR, the salience of ethnic identity was reinforced by the allocation of certain territories to specific ethnic groups based on more or less accurate historical claims. During the Soviet collapse, ethnic identity served as a powerful rallying tool, giving local elites enormous leverage in their battles with the center. Russia is the only post-Soviet state organized as a federation, but it still faces considerable challenges in defining the relationship among the various constituents of that federation. The war in Chechnya was a particularly brutal demonstration of these problems. At the same time, Tishkov and Olcott argue, Russia has made progress in enhancing the importance of citizenship over ethnicity, which creates some cause for optimism that interethnic antagonisms may diminish over time.

In their chapter, "Economic Reform Versus Rent Seeking," Anders Åslund and Mikhail Dmitriev investigate why the reform process has been so difficult in Russia. They refute the common view that the initial reforms were too radical, pointing out that Russia suffers not from unbridled capitalism but from excessive state intervention that impedes economic recovery. Although for many Russians the privatization of state assets has come to symbolize corruption, Åslund and Dmitriev point out that the big fortunes were not made on formal privatization but on government regulations and subsidies, as the early economic reformers lost out to those who wanted to make money on market distortions and government subsidies. Although the reformers made some headway, the structural adjustments they introduced were never sufficient—a shortcoming brought home forcefully by the financial crash of 1998. Åslund and Dmitriev see as major faults in the current economic system that the state tries to finance more than it can afford, that it is unable to carry out all social commitments, and that arbitrary and intrusive state regulation prevent the market from functioning as well as it could. All these features are reflections of a weak state. The question today is whether Russia will be able to introduce liberal capitalism or whether it will maintain the current crony capitalism.

Identity is also at the heart of what Sherman Garnett and Dmitri Trenin describe as Russia's difficulty in defining its foreign policy in "Russia and Its Nearest Neighbors." Russian military and political strategists have considerable trouble figuring out how to work with the new states that are their immediate neighbors. The authors offer a number of explanations for these problems, including the lingering paternalism of Soviet internal policy, the need for some forum in which Russia can demonstrate its claims to be a great power, and the uncertainty about Russia's goals in foreign policy. The most serious problem is the continuing conviction of Russia's leaders that their state is or should again become a great power—a conviction left unfulfilled by Russia's current weakness. A possibility of military adventurism arising from the desire for great-power recognition still exists, but the extent of the decline of Russia's military makes this unlikely. The bigger danger is Russia's continued preoccupation with its status and its attempts to use its relations with the Commonwealth of Independent States (CIS) to reinforce its own perceived image as a great power. While Russia hangs on to its old perceptions, its neighborhood is changing rapidly and decisively. Increasingly, weak CIS states—Tajikistan, Kyrgyzstan, Belarus, and Armenia—cling to Russia for support, but stronger neighbors, such as Uzbekistan and Ukraine, are forging new regional identities and orientations that make their status as former Soviet states increasingly irrelevant.

WHAT WE CONCLUDED

As this synopsis of the volume suggests, there is considerable variation in how the authors understand the common premises from which they began their work. Some of the difference can be explained by the diverse methodological approaches employed, the distinct intellectual perspectives of the authors, and the different disciplines that they represent.

As a result, there is significant divergence among the authors as to just how complete a transition Russia has undergone. All see the transformation as a fundamental one, but they differ over how much—or how little—has changed. Even Shevtsova and Olcott, who see Russia's failure to undergo a thorough elite transformation as detrimental to the development of democracy, admit that the same actors may be dominant in politics, but they are playing a new game, and with new (albeit not terribly) democratic rules. McFaul and Petrov look at the same political arena and offer a more optimistic set of conclusions—largely because they see the electoral process as likely to be sustained and intrinsically supportive of the development of democratic institutions.

The volume's authors express considerable concern as to whether the new Russian structures will endure. They voice several new worries. First, the Russian state is characterized by great weakness, which is reflected in all policy spheres. This emerges clearly in Åslund and Dmitriev's discussion of the economy. It is also a recurrent theme in Garnett and Trenin's discussion of Russia's foreign policy, especially as it relates to their nearest neighbors and former fellow countrymen. Second, several elements of a normal highly developed state are still strikingly absent, and in several cases, such as social services, it is not even clear that they are evolving. This is one of the themes that Åslund and Dmitriev stress as hindering reform in the economy. Finally, there is the question of the tenuousness of the psychological transition that has occurred since 1991. This point, too, comes up in a number of the essays. Tishkov and Olcott argue that until Russians start to think of themselves in civic and not solely ethnic terms, it will be difficult to resolve the contradictions implicit in Russian federalism. Moreover, as Garnett and Trenin make clear, this same ambiguity in worldview has clouded Russia's relations with the other newly independent states.

As a consequence, the chapters point to a large number of unresolved problems. Shevtsova and Olcott emphasize the rigidity of the elite structure; McFaul and Petrov describe Russia's failure to develop a democratic party system; Åslund and Dmitriev discuss the financial pitfalls faced by an only partly reformed economy; Tishkov and Olcott portray the continued division of society into competing ethnic groups; and Garnett and Trenin portray a Russia whose foreign policy goals frequently outstrip its capacity.

These concerns are all serious ones, but they need to be placed in the context of some good news as well. Today's Russia has an elected president. Although a democratic political party system is developing slowly, nationalist and other fringe groups have found it difficult to manage successfully the transition to electoral politics, while the Communist Party has problems attracting support from a younger generation. Even in a period of economic decline, there is little talk of returning to the old command-style economy. Nearly three years after Russia's withdrawal from Chechnya, the center and periphery continue to contest each other's claims to power and authority, but the competition seems almost certain to remain a peaceful one. The power of the Russian military continues to wane, but NATO enlargement went from a threat to a reality without a fundamental redefinition of U.S.–Russian strategic relations. While these relations were further strained in 1999 by the NATO engagement with Yugoslavia, even an angry Russian leadership is reluctant to return to a cold–war style engagement with the Americans.

All this points to the conclusion that the fundamental construction of a new society is already well under way. The shortcomings are likely to cause problems, but these will be the kinds of problems that the new Russia may well be able to handle. The future that the authors portray is less dramatic than many contemporary perceptions of Russia. Neither catastrophe nor paradise is being predicted. Certainly, a great deal has been accomplished in Russia's transformation to an independent state, a democracy, and a market economy. At the same time, however, Russia's postcommunist transformation remains incomplete in virtually all respects. The Russia of the future is still to be defined. The outcome depends on whether Russia manages to complete the fundamental transitions it has begun, or whether some link will turn out to be too weak and will warp the shape of the emerging structure.

While each pair of authors has a slightly different view of how developments in Russia are proceeding, one conclusion that we have all reached from our various vantage points is that the Russia emerging from well over seven years of transition is its own unique creation. The Russian economy is now responsive to market forces, but those in charge have had a great deal of flexibility in managing or limiting the transparency of the process. Political power remains consolidated in rather few hands, but the degree of popular empowerment exceeds that of any time in modern Russian or Soviet history. While the masses may yet make what outsiders consider to be inappropriate choices at the ballot box, the fear of mob rule is fading. While rule of law is still a tenuous and ill-defined ideal, basic civil rights and liberties seem relatively secure, at least in the overwhelmingly Russian regions. Russia still is not sure if it is an imperial or postimperial power; it fought a bloody war to hold on to Chechnya and still often looks at its new neighbors with paternal scorn, but it shows signs of growing less bellicose as its power recedes.

The Russia that has emerged is not the mirror-image of American or any other advanced Western form of democracy that some naive observers expected it to become almost instantly. Nor is it likely to turn into this any time soon. Yet, it is not the stripped-down and ideologically-sanitized version of the Soviet Union that many hostile observers predicted it would become either.

Russia is neither all black nor all white, and as a result it poses a challenge to Western policy makers who want both to stimulate the development of a democratic and market-oriented Russia and at the same time to encourage Russia's new neighbors to develop into all that they are capable of being. How to accomplish that remains a continuing challenge—one that many of the contributors to this volume deal with in their ongoing work.

For all of us involved with the Carnegie Moscow Center, it is enough to say that Russia has become a "normal" place. It is a place where we can all travel freely and do our research. It is a place where Russians and Americans can exchange ideas openly, and agree or disagree with one another with no dire consequence. It is a place to and from which we can send manuscripts back and forth across eight time zones by e-mail to put this book together—and one where we can sustain ourselves on the same bad fast food in Moscow as in Washington while we do it. It is a place that did not exist in anything like its current form when it was born out of the USSR's collapse in 1991, although it is obviously a place that draws deeply upon its Soviet and Russian pasts as well as on the experience of the West as it tries to reform its economy, restructure its political life, and revive its global stature.

In May 1999, as this book went to press, Boris Yeltsin dismissed Yevgeny Primakov as prime minister and nominated in his place Sergei Stepashin, the interior minister. The swift confirmation of Stepashin by the Duma, which followed the collapse of impeachment proceedings against the president in that body, seemed to be yet another in a series of improbable victories that Yeltsin has accumulated over the years. And yet, on the basis of the early evidence, the appointment of a new Russian government does not seem to change dramatically the possibility that Russia will soon resolve the serious political, economic, and foreign policy problems discussed in the chapters of this book. It does confirm, however, a point that is demonstrated in newspaper headlines virtually every day: that Russia is a country we need to understand better to make our own policies toward it more enlightened and productive.

1
Russia Transformed

Lilia Shevtsova and Martha Brill Olcott

Seven years after the collapse of the Soviet Union, Russia is still seeking to consolidate the institutional foundations of political pluralism, including a popularly elected legislature, the rule of law, an independent judiciary, civilian control of the military, and a constitution that embodies democratic principles which are accepted by government and society alike. Some of these institutional features are already in place. A substantial majority of Russian citizens participate in regularly held and widely contested elections for local and national representatives and also for the country's president. Freedom of expression is at an all-time high. A market economy is replacing centralized planning, and economic policy is overseen by a prime minister and cabinet who are nominated by the president and approved by the parliament.[1] While these elected and appointed officials may not always be responsive to popular demands, they are still the most accountable rulers in Russian history.

While the strides that Russia has made toward the establishment of a democratic regime are certainly impressive, the continued existence of a number of nondemocratic practices makes it clear that democracy is not Russia's only possible course. Some of these nondemocratic practices are likely to be transitional, while others are lingering vestiges of the communist past. Even some of the reformers who earlier were strong proponents of democratic change now talk about the risks inherent in democracies, making clear how incomplete Russia's democratic transition still remains.

Russia met one of the most basic tests of a democratic system in June 1996, when President Boris Yeltsin, then an unpopular incumbent, took the risk of public rejection by running in a contested election. Bold as this act may have been, both ironically and sadly, it did not resolve the contradictions still inherent in the country's incomplete political revolution.

Just as the election marathon was drawing to a close—at the very time when the population should have been able to draw confidence from its political leaders' commitment to election as the basis of presidential succession—the president faltered physically. Although political continuity was a major theme of the election campaign, Russia's voters were quickly stripped of the security that comes from electing an incumbent. Boris Yeltsin's heart ailment not only emphasized the weakness of his health, but it also served to underscore the fragility of Russia's democratic revolution. Instead of buying the country the time necessary to consolidate its political reforms, Yeltsin's victory created a host of new risks. Russians were faced with the prospect of a newly elected president too weak to carry reform further and so ill that he seemed unlikely to survive his term.

Though not a single scheduled election has yet been cancelled, Russia's political observers still view each new election with trepidation. Many fear that constitutionally mandated elections would not be held if Yeltsin were to die or become incapacitated before his term expires. Even if they are held, few in the Russian political establishment are confident that the next presidential election will be conducted as democratically as the already flawed previous one. Progovernment forces, radical reformers, communists, nationalists, and populists all claim that their opponents would be willing to manipulate democratic procedures either to gain or to keep power. All are worried about the same thing: that Russia's transition to democracy could be permanently derailed. Presidents who come to power extraconstitutionally rarely submit to popular judgment down the road, so members of each group fear that if they are excluded from power after Yeltsin leaves office, they may be indefinitely barred.

Fears that Russia will abandon its commitment to achieve political succession through competitive elections are fed by the hybrid nature of Russia's political system, in which newly created democratic institutions coexist with practices from the authoritarian past. This hybrid nature characterizes elite politics as well. The majority of the communist-era *nomenklatura* has managed to preserve some political power or to acquire new kinds of economic leverage, and even many of the younger new faces in elite circles come from formerly privileged Soviet families.[2] At the same time, the elite has been reconfigured into competing interest groups, making Russia's elite today far less homogeneous in its views than was its Soviet predecessor. New social groups are achieving representation in ruling circles, while some older members of the elite have fallen into disfavor or passed into voluntary retirement.

There is still no consensus among members of the ruling class about the nature of the political system they seek to build, much less agreement within the competing political groupings on how to achieve their diverse visions. Some of the groups make a priority of liberal economic reforms, assuming that the success of such policies will lead Russia to create and sustain a popularly supported pluralistic system. Others remain wedded to the idea of a militarily strong and resurgent Russia whose economic and political systems are both managed by the same small elite. While some of the nationalists among them support the idea of a twenty-first-century czar, others would like a red-brown coalition of nationalists and communists to recreate a Soviet-style vertically integrated bureaucratic system. Regional power holders have yet another view of how the state should be redefined: they seek a highly decentralized political system in which the localities are largely self-ruling, while still preserving a hierarchical style of decision making.

This lack of elite unanimity has weakened Russia, because each group seeks to vitiate the specific state institutions that most directly threaten its own conception of reform—and there is no agreement on which institutions should be strengthened to replace the more damaged existing ones. As a result, the restructuring of the state is proceeding more slowly than is the transformation of the political elite. The state remains Russia's single most important economic actor, and many in the political establishment continue to profit from it handsomely. While most of the Soviet-era state-owned and state-managed economic system has been formally dismantled, there is still the risk that a left-oriented government might reintroduce some of the mechanisms of a state-run and centrally managed economy. Even if this risk does not materialize, the various governments that Yeltsin has empowered have all exercised enormous influence in the economy, both through preferential treatment for powerful economic blocs and through the continued fusion (sometimes open, sometimes hidden) of the state with those who run the natural-resource monopolies and large financial-industrial groups.

Over the past several years, those who have tried to break up these monopolies to level the economic playing field have faced a frustrating uphill battle. Reformers who tried to do so from inside the government confronted fierce bureaucratic infighting, including efforts to besmirch their honesty, while private citizens were hampered by a legal system that still fails to protect the less powerful from those who are politically well connected.

The general weakness of the Russian state continues to slow the reform process as a whole, because powerful political interests often ignore constitutional provisions or parliamentary decrees that would restrict their freedom of action. At the same time, in a perverse way, the slowness with which economic reforms and political institutional development are proceeding is a source of some stability as well.

Many among the old Soviet elite were quite tolerant of the USSR's breakup, especially after the failed Communist Party coup in August 1991. Hundreds, if not thousands, of powerful men were able to transform political influence into access to economic goods by becoming well-paid managers or partial owners of raw materials, factories, or transport and communication services.

Dividing up the wealth of a country that comprises one-seventh of the earth's surface is a tricky procedure, especially when there are so many different and competing elite actors demanding their "fair share," not to mention the increasingly powerful new groups making their way to the bargaining table. The complexity of this task has helped slow the pace of both economic and political reform, especially now that there is an ailing president at the country's helm. Those who feel they have not yet received their fair share do not want to see the current arrangements finalized.

Whether the current incomplete quality of Russia's transformation is a good or bad thing for the nation is really unclear. It may be that the current political system, with its blending of quasi-democratic institutions with quasi-authoritarian values, provides just the continuity Russia needs to complete its transition from communism to a consolidated democracy. The quasi-democratic nature of the current political status quo, in combination with its weak institutional structures, gives all the major factions in the Russian political establishment hope that the present system can be manipulated to their own advantage. The cost of this stability, however, is that it gives no one an incentive to push Russia toward more democracy than it presently enjoys.

RUSSIA'S BUDDING BUT FLAWED DEMOCRACY

The most visible sign of the transformation of the Russian political system is that competitive elections have been held on a regular basis. In the first seven years of its post-Soviet existence, Russia has held one presidential election, two parliamentary elections, and several referenda and rounds of regional elections. (The June 1991 presidential election that brought Yeltsin to power took place some six months before the collapse of the Soviet Union.) In each case the results were accepted by winners and losers alike. Elections have been transformed from the empty ritual that they were in Soviet times to something fundamentally new. All of the major political factions, and even the groupings at the extreme ends of the political spectrum, have had enough confidence that the outcomes would be sustained that they chose to participate in all the various elections. In the 1995 parliamentary elections, for example, representatives of twenty-seven parties and political blocs (the majority of them rivals to Yeltsin's government) won seats.

For the first time, an important and unpredictable new player has been brought to Russia's political table—the population itself. Russia's voters now expect their government to listen to them in a way that they did not before the USSR broke apart. Russia's political culture is changing, and a sense of public accountability is beginning to affect Russia's ruling class. Survey data provide strong evidence of growing support for popularly elected democratic institutions. Research conducted in 1996 showed that the bulk of the Russian population—between 67 and 98 percent of those interviewed, depending upon their social status—agreed that the following statement of the fundamental principles of life is correct:

> "...the life of an individual is more important than any other consideration; laws should apply to everyone equally, from the president to the ordinary citizen; property is inviolable; the principal human rights are the right to life, to the defense of one's honor, and to civil liberties; freedom is as necessary to Russians as it is to people in the West."[3]

Russians appear to believe that their individual votes make a difference; voter turnout remains high throughout most of the country. More than two-thirds of the Russian population voted in the 1996 Russian presidential election: 69.7 percent and 68.8 percent of the potential electorate participated in the first and second rounds of balloting, respectively. By comparison, only 49 percent of *registered* voters cast ballots in the U.S. presidential election held the same year.

Some observers have tried to explain the continued high voter turnout as partially due to the inertia of an older generation long accustomed to the required voting of the Soviet era. Others ascribe it to the success of powerful local bosses, especially those in the countryside or in some of the national regions, who are particularly adept at organizing bloc voting by their constituents.

Yet neither of these explanations accounts for the fate of numerous incumbents at the ballot box. In the December 1995 elections to the Duma, for example, Russian voters unseated 71.6 percent of incumbents on party lists and 42.2 percent of those who ran on single-mandate district tickets; in the gubernatorial elections that were held during fall and winter 1996–1997, slightly more than half of the incumbents were defeated as well. Such figures suggest that the high voter turnout at Russia's elections is a reflection of the public's response to the real choices being offered them at the ballot boxes.

Turning incumbents out of office is just one sign of the growing sense of popular political entitlement. Russians also are becoming accustomed to the political freedoms that they have been granted, especially the right to the free expression of ideas. One poll conducted by the All-Russian Center for the Study of Public Opinion (VTsIOM) in September 1996, just after the presidential elections, showed that 57 percent of the Russians surveyed thought that the most positive change since 1985 has been the introduction of freedom of speech.[4]

These new political rights are exercised in a variety of ways, from greater openness in private settings, to increased opportunities for public demonstrations, to, most importantly, the expanded role of media in Russian life. There is also a wide range of new nongovernmental institutions through which citizens may transmit their dissatisfaction to legislative and government policy makers. The U.S. Agency for International Development alone has given technical assistance and grants to more than 300 Russian nongovernmental organizations serving as channels for citizen advocacy. This does not mean that most of these organizations are effective lobbying groups, or that the government is necessarily wary of the influence that they exercise, but it is nonetheless important that thousands of nongovernmental organizations have been registered all across Russia, that they are allowed to rent or own property, and that they are permitted to distribute their publications.

Many credit the growing number of nongovernmental organizations, especially the indigenous and foreign human rights advocacy and watchdog organizations that now work openly in Russia, with the substantial improvement in the protection of civil liberties and human rights that has occurred in the past decade. Nonetheless, the civil and human rights lobby remains small and fragmented. It is hampered by a weak and unpredictable legal system and is rarely able to move the Russian government when the government is hostile to its cause. Human rights groups were clearly far too weak to have had much impact on the conduct of the Chechnya War, which displaced half a million people and took more than fifty thousand civilian lives.[5] The brutality of this conflict, however, has made Russia's war-weary population potentially far more receptive to the arguments of human rights groups should a Chechnya-style standoff materialize in the future.

Human rights organizations may also take partial credit for the decision to move the Russian prison system from the jurisdiction of the Ministry of Internal Affairs to the supervision of the Ministry of Justice. Russian prisons were the subject of a critical Council of Europe report in May 1998, which complained that in some cases prison conditions were "tantamount to torture" because of extreme overcrowding, and that the "excessive use of arrest [was used] as a means of repression."[6]

Human rights groups were less successful in opposing the 1997 law on religion, which provided Russia's "traditional faiths" (the Orthodox church, Islam, Judaism, and Buddhism) with a special legal status, and consequently provided a legal foundation for discrimination against other organized religious groups. They have also had little success in rolling back observance of Soviet-era residence registration laws.[7] These have been strengthened by new legislation (even in Moscow) that violates the constitutional right of Russian citizens to freedom of movement, a right that has been upheld by the courts.

As troubling as these and other violations of constitutional and human rights are, they are nonetheless subject to a degree of public exposure and debate that was virtually impossible less than a decade ago. Much of the credit for this exposure belongs to Russia's mass media, the greatest single guarantor of an open public forum. The press is less free than it might be in ideal circumstances; its independence is often hampered by the media outlets' obligations to serve the political agendas of the business interests that finance them. But competition between these interest groups and between various media outlets is often keen. Newspapers and television broadcasters regularly take diametrically opposing positions on the leading political issues of the day. Aided as well by the lifting of most political and social taboos, the media has sponsored a spirited public discussion of ideas and issues as bold as it would be in any Western democracy.

Freedom of expression has produced enormous changes in Russia's political atmosphere, especially when combined with rights of public assembly. The Russian government must now regularly confront public challenges to unpopular policies as well as the risk that public demonstrations could get out of control. The substantial media attention given to strikes by unpaid workers and protests by pensioners, for example, was one of the factors that led President Yeltsin to abandon the reformers and their tight monetarist policies in the summer of 1998. Printing money to pay wage and pension arrears put further international financial support for Russia at great risk, but the government was even more worried that public protest might trigger mass civic unrest. (An earlier example was the government's eagerness to stabilize the situation in Chechnya before the 1996 presidential elections. There was little doubt that most Russian voters had wearied of this war far more rapidly than had the military leaders who were fighting it.)

Both the opposition and the Yeltsin government are beginning to learn what will drive people to the streets and how best to manipulate and respond to this. Neither camp, however, is as confident of predicting the behavior of ordinary Russians when they go to the ballot box, which is why elections produce far more tension in Russia than they do in Western democracies.

PROTECTING THE GOVERNMENT FROM THE PEOPLE

For many politicians the unpredictability of the electorate is easily translated into a distrust of the electoral process and the legislative bodies it produces. In established democracies, political incumbents may fear losing elections, but they do not fear that the basic rules that govern the political system will be fundamentally transformed if they are defeated. By contrast, Russia's political elite remains deeply distrustful of the electorate, fearing that a "wrong" outcome will lead to a wholesale rewriting of the rules of the game.

Such fears are not without foundation. Russian society today exhibits a sharp bipolarity between the communists and nationalists, on the one hand, and the pro-Westerners and market reformers on the other. In the middle is a large group of citizens who are still living in a state of political confusion as they try to assimilate the enormous changes their society has undergone. These people are highly susceptible to political manipulation.

All three groups are likely to consider themselves champions of democratic values, with each defining those values in rather different ways. As a result, many Russians may claim commitment to democracy and still vote for Communist Party candidates, or alternatively may transfer their allegiance from Communist to nationalist candidates because they see the latter as better advocates of popular empowerment. Russians may also claim that they are for the protection of private property (by which they mean the right to own their own home or to run a small business) even as they oppose the policies of the liberal market reformers because they call for the privatization of all the country's assets. Western observers may see Russia's leading young reformers as "democrats," but many Russian voters accuse these people of having turned over Russia's resources to "crooks," and blame them for the declining standard of living and the growing problems of crime and corruption. These voters believe themselves to be as democratic as anyone else, but they would like to have the old social privileges combined with the new political rights. They believe that Russia's leaders must address the fact that ordinary citizens have lost more over the past seven years than they have gained, and so they feel better protected by politicians whom Westerners and liberal market-oriented reformers consider antidemocratic.

Those around President Yeltsin and the liberal market reformers are more fearful of the electorate than are either the communists or the nationalists. The latter two groups see support of the electorate as their best chance of gaining political power, and the fact that both have fared well in legislative elections in particular helps explain why President Yeltsin has sought to strengthen the executive branch at the expense of the legislative.

The fears of these people are reflected in the present constitution, which was written in late 1993, after the dramatic October 1993 storming of the Soviet-era parliament (whose leaders had barricaded themselves inside to protest what they understood to be Yeltsin's illegal exercise of power). The October events convinced Yeltsin's government that presidential power had to be protected from interference by the legislature. As a result, supporters of the president drafted a constitution that assigned the preponderance of the country's formal powers to the presidency. The president is effectively the head of state and the head of government. He appoints the prime minister and the members of the cabinet and has the right to dissolve the Duma if it rejects his candidate for prime minister three times. The president also has extensive rights to rule through decree and has the responsibility for appointing many of the country's senior jurists.

The constitution was designed to insulate the government from the will of the people or their representatives. According to Article 108, the passage of ordinary amendments or federal constitutional laws requires a two-thirds majority in the lower house, a concurring three-quarters majority in the upper house, and the president's signature. The signed amendment then needs to be ratified by two-thirds of the legislative assemblies of the country's *oblasts* and autonomous regions.[8] This gives representatives of the regional bureaucracy the opportunity to block proposed changes to the constitution as well.

The current constitution also insulates the president from suffering the effects of public or legislative displeasure. It is virtually impossible to remove the president from office. Impeachment, which can only be initiated for high treason or "other grave crimes" (a category so vague as to be nearly meaningless), requires a two-thirds majority in both houses of the Federal Assembly plus the approval of the Supreme and Constitutional Courts—all of which must be completed within three months.

This concentration of power in presidential hands did not make Russia's parliament so weak as to be irrelevant. Although Russia's legislators play a far smaller role than they would like in policy making, and a smaller one than their colleagues do in most other democratic systems, the Russian legislature is more than a rubber stamp for the president (unlike its counterparts in a number of other post-Soviet states). Moreover, the role of legislators has increased as Russia's economic crisis has deepened. In autumn 1997, for example, they were granted a rather token role during the budget war between the government and the parliament. At that time Yeltsin's negotiations with the communist opposition led to the formation of the so-called Council of Four (the president, the prime minister, and the speaker of each house of parliament). The deal also resulted in an agreement to convene roundtable meetings to discuss important policy issues with leaders of the opposition and other legislative representatives, although this consultative body generally played a symbolic rather than an active role in policy making. In March–April 1998, President Yeltsin was forced to make a major lobbying effort with the Duma to gain approval for Sergei Kiriyenko as prime minister. Once again, however, Yeltsin's concessions to the leaders of the legislature were more face-saving than substantive.

The situation began to change rapidly with the ruble's collapse in the summer of 1998. The Kiriyenko government initially pressed the Duma to raise Russia's debt ceiling, but when his policies failed to stabilize the ruble, the leaders of the Duma choose to press their powers to their constitutional limit to test presidential authority.

Twice rejecting Viktor Chernomyrdin, Yeltsin's choice for prime minister, the Duma leaders effectively convinced the Russian president that in the face of their inevitable third rejection he had better choose a new candidate from *their* list. The alternative was the disbanding of the Duma, an act that might well have pushed a deeply troubled country into the abyss economically and politically. That would have left Yeltsin and his advisors with the choice of either holding new elections or sponsoring some sort of palace coup, possibly with the help of General Lebed.

In the end, Yeltsin chose to withdraw the nomination of Chernomyrdin in favor of that of Yevgeny Primakov, then foreign minister, whose rapid confirmation provided a peaceful exit from a dangerous deadlock. Unfortunately, the government that Primakov formed had few ready solutions for Russia's economic meltdown and was generally seen by reformers as a step backward.[9]

Yet the decision to appoint Primakov remains an important one. It demonstrated once again that Yeltsin and his opponents were still striving to find peaceful solutions in times of crisis and that both recognize that an unresolved crisis could lead to a popularly supported extraconstitutional seizure of power. These instances of cooperation between the president and the legislature are difficult to arrange in a political climate that does not encourage sustained and regular communication between the two branches of government. President Yeltsin typically only turns to the legislature when confronted with looming economic catastrophe, strikes, or the threat of large public demonstrations. In fact, until the appointment of Yevgeny Primakov as prime minister, the government sought to draft legislation with only minimal consultation with the Duma because of the difference in the two branches' philosophies of reform.

With the exception of Primakov's period as prime minister, relations between Russia's legislative and executive branches have varied from mildly hostile to extremely confrontational. Since October 1993, however, neither side has been willing to take the risks associated with pressing for maximum advantage. In the many crisis situations that have developed, neither the Duma nor the government has shown an appetite for early parliamentary elections. The Communist bloc, which dominates the Duma, has a strong incentive to avoid dissolution, since the next election may well demonstrate that its popularity has diminished. During the autumn 1998 crisis, the president also chose to retreat from a direct confrontation with parliament. Russia is still a long way from the regular consultation between the legislative and executive branches that characterizes politics in most developed democracies. But the fact that the president and the Duma have each been willing to retreat when confronted with emergency or near emergency situations lays the groundwork for expanding the limited political dialogue that currently exists between these competing forces.

Russia's current institutional arrangements provide few real incentives for the development of mass political parties, which further insulates those governing from organized expressions of the popular will. In the absence of a strong parliament there is little incentive for strong parties to develop, and most Russian parties still play a largely ceremonial role. Even the introduction of a party list system in the Duma elections (an innovation that helped stimulate party development in other countries after World War II) did little to mobilize the Russian population to support either the nascent progovernment or the proreform parties in the 1993 and 1995 elections.[10]

Nationalists and communists have fared somewhat better in their efforts to organize political parties. The latter, in particular, have benefited from decades of organizational experience. Neither the antigovernment nor the progovernment reformers, though, has ever managed to develop a political platform that captured the public imagination. The failure of Yeltsin's administration to form a governing party has led it to create conditions that further hamper the process of political party development, to keep the opposition from gaining political advantage.

The existence of a stronger legislature would provide a real incentive for political groups to dedicate more time, thought, and money to the arduous process of forming mass parties. Their absence denies most Russian citizens something enjoyed by their counterparts in developed democracies: a means of conveying their will to their elected representatives.

GOVERNMENT FOR THE GOVERNORS

The end result of all of this is a political system in which the population is not well represented. Those in charge of Russia's political institutions are not as accountable to the public as they would be in a consolidated democracy. In fact, most Russians still believe that the government is more interested in serving the needs of the governing class than the needs of the people at large. This encourages people to use demonstrations, strikes, and other forms of protest to get the government to recognize their needs.

The weakness of the party system and the limited powers of the Duma have exacerbated Russia's social problems. They have also created few incentives for sound policy making. Stripped of the power to initiate legislation, deputies (particularly opposition deputies) use the Duma floor to make rhetorical statements or exaggerated policy demands that are aimed at the crowd. This has helped further incite the population to public protest and has increased the pressure on the president and his government to turn governing into a form of crisis management, especially in the social sphere. Efforts by some of Yeltsin's early economic reform cabinets to develop the state's medium- and long-term capacity to meet its public obligations, for example, were criticized by most ordinary Russians as limiting social welfare benefits during a time of growing economic hardship.

The growing gap between rich and poor is oftentimes a visible one, given the pervasively public nature of Russia's new consumer culture. The fact that many of the new have-nots are the anonymous heroes of the Soviet system—soldiers, miners, bus drivers, teachers, rural doctors, and others who lived comparatively comfortable lives under the communist system—only serves to compound the problem. The anger of these newly socially degraded groups is further fueled by the frequent charges of corruption made against figures in and around the governing groups, and by revelations of the soft landings that most of those who get pushed out of power have managed to engineer for themselves.

The weakness of Russia's legal system only helps to foster the widespread perception that members of the elite use public service as a vehicle for advancing their private business interests.[11] Many ordinary Russians also believe that those serving in the police and other security forces condone official abuses of power or participate directly in criminal activities. The weakness of the court system combined with the ineffectiveness of well-intentioned law enforcement officials has forced a considerable portion of the Russian population to resort to semilegal or illegal means to gain protection and to seek redress of their grievances.

The failure to institutionalize principles of the rule of law has made it harder to distinguish between honest and dishonest politicians. Prominent figures who are accused of improprieties or crimes wind up being "tried" and either "convicted" or "acquitted" by the press, since they are unable to clear their names in court. The prevailing atmosphere of disregard for the rule of law also hampers democracy building by encouraging most ordinary citizens to flout the law as energetically as does the elite. Probably the most egregious example of this is tax collection: according to the State Tax Service, only 16 percent of the 2.6 million taxpaying legal entities (people and enterprises) in Russia pay their taxes in full. Fifty percent pay some of their taxes, and 34 percent pay no taxes at all.[12] Widespread tax evasion has impeded the government's ability to meet social welfare payments, combat crime, and maintain public order. Without question, tax evasion also contributed to Russia's dire economic crisis in the summer of 1998.

The short-lived Kiriyenko government (March–August 1998) launched a massive nationwide effort to improve tax collection. But while the young prime minister's approach may have been correct from an economic point of view, the fact that it was not adopted until mid-1998 effectively doomed it to defeat. Revenues simply could not be raised quickly enough to stabilize the ruble or to increase government spending at a rate sufficient to increase public approval of the government.

The Yeltsin administration understood that the decision to abandon tight currency controls and the strategy of a largely market-driven economic reform (which were implicit in the decision to appoint Yevgeny Primakov as prime minister) meant that critical international financial support would be difficult to retain. But it also understood that the alternative—supporting the reformers but disbanding the government— brought with it the risk of provoking sufficient popular unrest to threaten the regime's ouster. This would have been true whether Boris Yeltsin chose to rule by decree or parliamentary elections were held and an even more unmanageable Duma replaced the current one.

That Yeltsin opted for the least confrontational course should not be surprising. For all the talk of its undemocratic tendencies, the Yeltsin government has in fact tried to minimize its use of the extraordinary powers granted to the presidency by the 1993 constitution. Certainly in the one big "democratic" choice that Russia faced since independence—the decision to hold the 1996 elections as scheduled—the government proceeded as public law demanded, in spite of the fact that Yeltsin's popularity was dangerously low at the time.

This does not mean that the Yeltsin team is not willing to take extralegal steps to minimize its political risk. Numerous complaints of unfair election practices levied against the Yeltsin camp speak to the sliding scale of fairness that was applied in that election. To be sure, the criteria that make an election free and fair are contentious even in settings that are more democratic than Russia's. In the United States, for example, some candidates inevitably have larger war chests than do their opponents. And in those Western democracies with strict campaign finance laws, progovernment parties generally have an easier time gaining media endorsements than do antigovernment ones. Nonetheless, despite the fact that Russia's 1996 presidential election was well monitored by international observers, there were numerous complaints that the government had tampered with the electoral process to ensure a favorable outcome. Among the most frequent accusations was that the Yeltsin campaign seriously violated the spending limit of approximately $3 million set by the Central Electoral Commission. The far larger war chest of Yeltsin's team permitted his campaign to overwhelm Gennady Zyuganov, the Communist Party candidate, with both the quantity and the quality of its political advertising. The Yeltsin team was able to draw on the skills of some of the best image makers available, while the Zyuganov group had neither the money nor the imagination to mount a comparable campaign.

International observers also voiced concern about the apparent media bias in favor of the incumbent. According to the European Mass Media Institute (EMMI), President Yeltsin received more than 52 percent of the television news coverage, while Zyuganov, his main rival, received only 18 percent. While fear of a return to communist rule and censorship gave media organizations strong incentives to slant coverage in Yeltsin's favor,[13] EMMI also noted that senior media figures were reported to be receiving generous retainers from the Yeltsin campaign to guarantee their loyalty, and even junior journalists were said to have received compensation for positive stories about the Russian president.[14]

What may prove more important for the development of Russian democracy, however, is that even Yeltsin's remarkable success in the 1996 election did not make those in his political camp more confident of the reliability of the Russian electorate. Yeltsin's physical collapse during the summer of 1996, followed by his repeated bouts of ill health, have made those in his inner circle even less secure than they were before.

The presidency is still at the center of Russian political life, and given the weakness of so many other political institutions, personal loyalty to the president is even more important than is fealty to the state or adherence to the law. All of Russia now lives under the constant threat that if Yeltsin's health fails, new elections will be called before the country's economic problems are solved and a leader acceptable to the political establishment is ordained. This has tied the vitality of the political system to the physical condition and mental capacity of the leader. Yeltsin's poor health has left the country in a permanent succession struggle and has stimulated fears that the rules of the whole game, not simply the political course, might soon be changed.

Yeltsin's rapid physical collapse has made it harder for the 1996 presidential election to become a precedent if Yeltsin should die or become incapacitated. This uncertainty, combined with the weakness of the legislative and judicial system, has led to the formation of political coteries that are able to exercise the authority of the presidency during his growing periods of relative incapacity. Even when a healthy Boris Yeltsin is at the center of this system, most of the important political debate still goes on in and around the presidential court. This court behavior trickles down through Russian society, as nepotism, clannish struggles, and insider deals become permanent features of Russian politics. Even the media is now more controlled than before the 1996 elections, due to the continued need for competing elite groups to manipulate the press for partisan purposes.

Boris Yeltsin is Russia's first president, and is a democratically elected one. The ways in which he exercises the direct and delegated powers of his office create important precedents for the Russian political system far into the future. While all key groups of the political establishment continue to endorse the principle of succession through election, the likelihood that future elections will occur at all seems to depend in large part on how the current governing political elite views its prospects of preventing "antisystem" forces from winning future elections and then changing the rules of the game.

STASIS OR STAGNATION?

It is too soon to predict with confidence the long-term stability of Russia's current form of government or whether its authoritarian aspects will eventually undermine the more democratic ones. In theory, Russia's hybrid regime should have become increasingly unstable with the passage of time. In fact, however, the country's mix of disparate and even contradictory features has weathered some severe crises. Like Yeltsin himself, the system seems to hang on to life against the odds.

The current blend of a quasi-pluralistic society and a quasi-authoritarian presidency has helped facilitate Russia's largely peaceful transition from a vast empire to a much smaller and less powerful multinational state. This mix of old and new has helped the Russian polity weather periodic political crises. The increasingly heterogeneous nature of the Russian elite facilitates greater debate on policy issues prior to the government taking decisions. It also allows the government to reverse itself over time. This is helped by the fact that the Russian government is made up of an astounding mix of interests: over time liberals, conservatives, democrats, communists, left-wing centrists, "great power" advocates, and populists have all been chosen to fill key positions in the government and in its consultative organs. Sometimes they have served simultaneously, at other times, sequentially. In general, the clash of competing interests is a good thing, especially since many disagreements among elites are being played out in the open for the first time in post-Soviet politics.

The negative side of this is that there are still no firm agreements on rules to ensure the inclusion of multiple interests (a situation that Boris Yeltsin has been able to use to his advantage).[15] Russia's political establishment offers a sufficiently rich mix of personnel for the government to find convincing spokesmen for almost every position in the country's political spectrum. The choice is so great that the Kremlin is able to behave like a chameleon and to alternate its political hue to protect itself from virtually any challenge to its authority. This flexibility has allowed Yeltsin's team to draw former critics into government at different times and to offer continually changing responses to emerging crises within the country. The fluidity of government positions on key issues has also made it more difficult for an effective opposition to develop.

The current system has placed a premium on political fire fighting and consensus building rather than on introducing systematic reforms that might redress the original source of conflict. Such behavior strengthens the power of the president, who acts as the supreme arbiter among powerful, competing groups, and permits a relatively benign release of potentially explosive pressure that might otherwise be fatally damaging to the regime.

Yeltsin's strategy has succeeded in insulating the presidency from the preeminence of any one of the competing ideologies that still dominate Russia's political life. It is less clear whether his actions will allow for the orderly transfer of power to a successor and, eventually, to a new political generation. Yeltsin's early 1998 cabinet shuffle and his repeated elevation of young newcomers to the national political stage are important steps in the cultivation of future leaders. At the same time, the president's continued vacillation between competing interests—which was so marked in his September 1998 switch from young reformers to Gorbachev-era economic planners—has left younger politicians feeling extremely vulnerable.

Instead of being relieved each time a political crisis is resolved, Russia's political class immediately begins to fear what will happen the next time presidential intervention is required. Though Yeltsin increasingly appears too sick to rule, he has repeatedly refused to resign. But Yeltsin's incapacity to govern creates a number of critical problems. Among these is whether the powers of the presidency can be transferred informally and temporarily to the prime minister, or whether they will continue to rest with a presidential entourage that is able to act in Yeltsin's name but without his supervision.

Public discussion about limiting the president's vast powers has occurred with greater frequency since the financial crises of 1998 revealed that the health of Russia's economy had become as fragile as that of its president. Many in Russia's political establishment are as frightened by the prospect of a Yeltsin succession as they are by the risks associated with a weak president remaining in office. Their primary concern is that if Yeltsin should die or resign before his term expires, a new president could use the vast powers of the office to create a dictatorship—something Boris Yeltsin, to his credit, refrained from doing.

While Yeltsin has so far managed to fight off any formal power-sharing arrangements, competing power centers are learning to be more effective in challenging him. This was vividly demonstrated when the legislature successfully pressed Yeltsin to withdraw Chernomyrdin's nomination as prime minister in September 1998. Yevgeny Primakov's ability to turn the post of prime minister into one that functions as a sort of vice president or acting president was another successful institutional challenge.

Russia's governors and republic presidents have also become adept at inflating their powers to protect their respective regional interests. During the economic crisis of 1998 they brazenly withheld taxes and embargoed locally produced goods to try to sustain the living standards of their populations. The strongest of these regional leaders—who include Yuri Luzhkov (the mayor of Moscow) as well as Aleksandr Lebed (the governor of Krasnoyarsk)—are likely to be serious candidates to replace Boris Yeltsin.

Yeltsin also had reasonable success playing many of these leaders off against each other, using the asymmetric statuses of the administrative units that they govern to his advantage as well. In addition to being regulated by the constitution, center-periphery relations in Russia have also been defined by a series of bilateral treaties.[16] Most of these were negotiated and executed behind closed doors by regional leaders and the Russian president (who chose not to involve the Federal Parliament). Many observers see the arrangement as a potential source of instability, and they are particularly critical of the treaties signed with the strongest regions, all of which violate core provisions of the federal constitution.[17] For now, the center is too weak to renege on these treaty commitments, although these deals could well come to haunt Yeltsin's successor.

The atmosphere of conciliation is further stimulated by the fact that virtually no elements in the current ruling elite, no matter how they may squabble among themselves, are interested in overthrowing the regime. The memory of the violent denouement of October 1993 still leaves most political groups willing to moderate their passions rather than to risk drawing society into a conflict that might spin out of control. Those same memories also help reinforce stability in Russia from below. Having lived through more than a decade of tumultuous political transition, people are now demanding an end to upheavals and disruptions in their lives.

The presidential elections in 1996 communicated exactly this message. At that time voters appeared to be afraid that any radical change would only worsen the situation. Even those voters who had not benefited from life under Yeltsin revealed their aversion to promises of revolution and programs for change by reelecting the incumbent.[18] Political leaders who advocated radical shifts were unpopular and unelectable. That this change in public attitudes had a real impact on the Russian Communist Party is a case in point. After failing to win the presidency in 1996, party leaders responded by shedding the organization's most radical members and by trying to appeal to moderate, nonrevolutionary sentiment as they prepared for subsequent elections in Russia's regions.

Russia's current level of stability, however, may not prove durable. Stability that is neither grounded in economic growth nor in the trust of democratic institutions usually proves to be short-lived, and oftentimes serves as the genesis of political or economic crisis.

Millions of people have lost out in the transition from the old Soviet Union to the new Russia. Russia's current political institutions have been designed to make it difficult for popular protest to oust the government, let alone to change the nature of the regime. The country's political forces are not frozen in time; a few small changes could ignite a volatile mix. These might include the emergence of a charismatic leader who commands strong support among the politically estranged white-collar class that lost its savings (and hope for the future) during the financial crisis of 1998, disgruntled miners and workers in the energy sector, or even underpaid military forces.

If economic conditions continue to deteriorate, even smaller scale protests could prove destabilizing, especially if they are handled ineptly. In the absence of strong political parties or other well-organized interest groups, spontaneous antigovernment actions could escalate quickly. This is something that most in Russia's political establishment remain quite sensitive to and will try to take deliberate steps to control, even if this means temporarily suspending Russia's new political freedoms.

CONCLUSION

In less than a decade, the Russian Federation has transformed the political system it inherited after the collapse of the Soviet Union into something radically different. Both the governing class and the population have come to accept the legitimacy of such new concepts and institutions as competitive elections, free speech, representative governmental bodies, and the right to hold private property. At the same time, a democratic political system is neither fully developed nor securely entrenched in Russia. Holdover values and practices from the communist past undermine open and fair competition, popular participation, and respect for individual rights. Russia still has limited experience with important aspects of private property rights, lacks a well-developed tradition of the rule of law, has a small middle class, has an even smaller but much more powerful new economic elite, and lives with a set of unresolved social and ethnic conflicts.

The enthusiasm of earlier years for democratic reform is now waning among many in the ruling establishment. The new Russian elite has established a secure system that preserves its power and wealth; it is now primarily interested in protecting these things. At the same time, society's growing aversion to radical change and the public's demand for greater order and protection reduce popular pressure for further democratization.

This does not mean that a return of authoritarianism is inevitable. Among the factors that work to inhibit its return are the inability of any political group to gain a monopoly of power; the absence of an efficient bureaucracy or a loyal and capable army at the center of Russia; and the growing power of regional elites who do not wish to see their positions undermined by the center. Finally, there is a growing awareness among competing elite groups that authoritarianism means isolation and that the country will not survive if it remains outside the world community.

The current hybrid nature of Russia's political system leaves the nation vulnerable to the risk of a return to authoritarianism or the emergence of oligarchic rule. These risks will remain until the political system is transformed into one in which an independent legislature or judiciary is able to respond effectively to the excesses of presidential power. Any form of balance of power assumes the possibility of sharing power by opposing groups within the political elite. Many in Russia still fear that their country's political culture has not yet evolved far enough to support the existence of a responsible empowered opposition.

Key members of Russia's governing elite still seem to believe that it is more important who will rule than how that ruler comes to power. In 1996 it was their view that a duly elected communist or nationalist president who ruled over an empowered parliament dominated by his own party would pose a greater risk to the future of Russian democracy than a democratic-minded president who came to power by undemocratic means. Fortunately, Boris Yeltsin ultimately rejected their advice and chose to run for the presidency, but there is little to suggest that the mindset of Russia's elite has changed. So long as Russia's political class struggles with this kind of dilemma, Russian politics will be dominated by individuals rather than institutions, and Russian democracy will remain incomplete and unconsolidated.

NOTES

[1] The Russian parliament, called the Federal Assembly, is made up of the Federation Council (upper house) and the State Duma (lower house). The Duma must approve presidential appointments of the prime minister and other high-level ministers.

[2] The term *nomenklatura* refers to the people who made up the traditional communist elite, namely managers, enterprise owners, bureaucrats, and advisers to the president.

[3] *Nezavisimaya gazeta*, January 16, 1997.

[4] *Moskovskii komsomolets*, October 14, 1996.

[5] U. S. Department of State, Bureau of Democracy, Human Rights, and Labor, *1996 Human Rights Report: Russia* (Washington, D.C.: U. S. Department of State, January 30, 1997).

[6] *RFE-RL Daily Reports*, May 19, 1998 (Radio Free Europe/Radio Liberty, Prague, Czech Republic).

[7] U. S. Department of State, Bureau of Democracy, Human Rights, and Labor, *1997 Human Rights Report: Russia* (Washington, D.C.: U. S. Department of State, January 30, 1998).

[8] The Russian Federation is made up of various types of political entities. As of the beginning of 1998, it included 21 republics (*respubliki*), six territories (*kraia*), 49 regions (*oblasti*), one Jewish autonomous region (*avtonomnaiya oblast*), ten autonomous areas (*avtonomniye okruga*), and two "cities of federal importance," namely Moscow and St. Petersburg.

[9] Much to the dismay of proponents of reform in Russia, Primakov awarded two of the country's highest economic posts to Soviet-era thinkers. Yury Maslyukov, who was appointed first deputy prime minister in charge of the economy, had been chief of Gos-Plan under Gorbachev; Viktor Geraschenko, the new chairman of the Central Bank, had been a banker in the Soviet period and held the post of Central Bank chairman from 1992 to 1994. Other top ministers in Primakov's government include Foreign Minister Igor Ivanov, a close associate of Primakov's during the latter's tenure as foreign minister; Defense Minister Igor Sergeyev, who has held

that position since May 1997; Interior Minister Sergei Stepashin, who also retains his previous position; and Finance Minister Mikhail Zadornov, who is considered to be a reformer but whose work in previous governments has earned him partial blame for the current crisis. Biographical information on Russian ministers is from the web site of the Russia Today news service (www.russiato day.com/rtoday/special/minister.html).

10 The Russian Duma, or lower house of parliament, is elected through two procedures. Half of the 450 deputies are elected by party lists in a system of proportional representation; parties that acquire more than 5 percent of the vote take the number of seats that corresponds to their popularity in the vote. The other 225 seats are contested locally in single-mandate constituencies.

11 On this general problem, see Iakov Pappe, "Otraslevye lobbi v pravitel'stve Rossii," *Pro et Contra*, Fall 1996, pp. 61–79.

12 "Prezidentskaiya administratsiya obnaruzhila nesostoiatel'nost' nalogovoi sistemy," *Segodnya*, February 5, 1997, pp. 1, 3.

13 Even the independent television network NTV, which had developed a reputation for being extremely critical of the president and his policies, began to devote an inordinate amount of positive coverage to Yeltsin during the electoral campaign.

14 U. S. Department of State, Bureau of Democracy, Human Rights, and Labor, *1996 Human Rights Report: Russia* (Washington, D.C.: U.S. Department of State, January 30, 1997), Section 2, "Respect for Civil Liberties."

15 Of course, the inclusion of incompatible interests in the government has also backfired, leading to intense clashes that extend well beyond the circle of leaders. Aleksander Rutskoi's tenure in the government as Russia's first (and to date only) vice president, for example, ended in a violent social explosion. But the regime coped much more smoothly with another maverick, Aleksander Lebed, after he was brought into the government and not long thereafter began to clash with other members of the ruling elite.

16 On the various treaties that the president has signed with the regional centers, see James Hughes, "Moscow's Bilateral Treaties Add to Confusion," *Transition*, September 20, 1996, pp. 39–43.

17 For a discussion of this problem, see Vladimir Lysenko, "Power Sharing and the Experience of the Russian Federation," paper presented at a Carnegie Corporation conference on "Preventing

Deadly Conflict: Strategies and Institutions," Moscow, August 14–16, 1996.

[18] By all accounts, Yeltsin ran a brilliantly effective campaign that identified this mood in the electorate and then capitalized on it by emphasizing preservation of the status quo. Surely this served the elite's interest in preserving a system of power that it had been protecting since the Soviet Union's collapse.

2

The Changing Function of Elections in Russian Politics

Michael McFaul and Nikolai Petrov

Since 1989, Russian citizens have voted often. There have been four parliamentary elections (1989, 1990, 1993, and 1995); two presidential elections (1991 and 1996); four referenda (two in 1991, two in 1993); three rounds of elections for regional legislatures (1990, 1993–1994, 1996); and three rounds of elections for regional heads of administration (the first in 1991–1992 for republics and in 1993 for *oblasts* and *krais*, the second in 1995, and the third in the fall of 1996).[1] These frequent elections have performed a somewhat different function in Russia's democratization process than have elections in other countries making a similar transition. Three paradoxes are most salient. First, Russian elections have produced neither a change of power at the national level nor a complete replacement of political leaders from the Soviet era. Second, these elections have not stimulated the formation of a multiparty system. Third, the electoral process has not become more transparent or more competitive over time. In many ways, electoral procedures in Russia were less free and fair in 1996 than they were in 1990.

Why have elections in Russia not produced the same patterns and results they have produced in other young democracies? In answering this question, we reject claims of any Russian historical or cultural uniqueness in this respect. Russian voters are not genetically predisposed to vote against their interests, culturally hindered in organizing parties, or historically prone to corruption. Instead, we argue that the function of elections in Soviet and then Russian politics can only be understood when placed within the larger context of Russia's unfolding political and economic transformation. Unlike transitions to democracy in Latin America and Southern Europe, the transition from Soviet communist rule was not only about the crafting of new democratic institutions. Negotiations over the new rules of the game for the political system occurred at the same time the Soviet command economy was being transformed into a market system and the Soviet state itself was being dissolved. In this context of rapid and simultaneous change of both political and economic institutions, leaders from the Soviet ancien régime and Russian challengers to the old order became polarized into two political camps. In contrast to negotiated transitions to democracies in other parts of the world, these two camps failed to agree on a new set of political rules. Instead, in a polarized standoff in August 1991 and again in October 1993, these opposing political forces solved their differences not through negotiations but conflict and eventually armed struggle.[2]

In this kind of transition, elections were not the goals or objectives of the political conflict but the means for obtaining other ends. During much of the electoral history discussed in this chapter, the goal of consolidating democratic institutions was less important to most actors than securing or impeding economic transformation or promoting or blocking Russian independence. Boris Yeltsin and his allies used elections to gain political power as a means of pursuing their more central goals of economic transformation and Soviet dissolution. Consequently, elections have not yet played the same positive force for the development of democratic institutions and practices in Russia as they have in other countries.

This chapter begins with a description of the general function that elections have played in transitions to democracy throughout the world, and then explains how the Russian experience has diverged from these general patterns. We then describe briefly all major national elections for public office from 1989 to 1996, and summarize the general patterns of Russia's nascent electoral history. The chapter concludes with some predictions about the continuing evolution of the Russian electoral system.

ELECTIONS IN TRANSITIONS TO DEMOCRACY

In most transitions to democracy, the successful completion of a series of elections produces the following results:

First, electoral support for the "founding fathers" wanes. In the first or founding elections, challengers of the old regime tend to score dramatic electoral victories. In the next set of elections, the romantic era of transition usually ends, since the expectations that voters formed during the transition are never fully met. This reaction against the new leaders has proven especially acute in transitions from communist rule, in which political transformation is usually accompanied by a painful economic transformation.

Second, the successful completion of several electoral cycles in democratic transitions usually stimulates the development of political parties.[3] Founding elections tend to offer the largest number of choices to voters. Over time, however, these numbers dwindle as parties that do not win representation disappear. Voters also gradually learn what these parties stand for and become less likely to waste votes on fringe parties.[4] While declining in number, parties tend to increase in importance after a democratic transition, as they emerge to play the central role intermediating interests between state and society. Every stable democracy in the world has a party system.

Third, the successful completion of several elections tends to make the electoral process more democratic. Because they are new events, founding elections in democratic transitions often are marred by irregularities. Outgoing dictators wield control of the state apparatus to falsify results and to terrorize voters. Often, first elections are deliberately not fully democratic, but instead serve as an interim step between dictatorship and democracy. Over time, however, these constraints on and irregularities in the democratic process fade. Practice makes perfect.

After several years of elections, however, Russia still does not seem to be following any of these general trends.

First, electoral support for opposition parties and candidates—whether they are communists, national-patriots, or opposition democrats—has not grown dramatically. Instead, those who won during Russia's first elections have continued to stay in power. This sustained support for Russia's founding fathers was demonstrated most dramatically in the 1996 presidential election, when Boris Yeltsin became the first incumbent in the postcommunist world to win reelection in a relatively free and fair election. This result was especially surprising considering all that Russians had endured during Yeltsin's five-year tenure: dramatic economic decline, a brief civil war in Moscow in 1993, the prolonged war in Chechnya, and significant increases in crime. In 1996 opinion polls revealed that most people thought they were better off under communism than under the present system.[5]

Second, Russia's party system has not consolidated over time: there are still too many ineffective parties and not enough effective parties. In 1990 two effective protoparties competed in parliamentary elections. In 1993 thirteen parties competed. In 1995, amazingly, forty-three parties competed. Only four, however, achieved the 5 percent threshold required to win seats in parliament. And even these four parties have poor records of representation—and uncertain electoral futures. Only the Communist Party resembles a real, national party that is likely to outlive its current leaders. Yabloko (the liberal opposition party headed by Grigory Yavlinsky) and Our Home Is Russia (the "party of power" headed by former prime minister Viktor Chernomyrdin) have little grassroots support. Vladimir Zhirinovsky's Liberal Democratic Party of Russia (LDPR) does have an extensive network of regional offices and local organizers, but it remains unclear whether this organization is a genuine party or a movement based on a cult figure. Strikingly, in both national and regional elections not organized by proportional representation, only the Communist Party has played a central role in influencing outcomes.

Third, Russian electoral procedures have not become more democratic over time. Expectations about electoral fraud or postponement were much lower in 1990 or 1991 than they were in 1995 or 1996. In fact, the specter of postponement lingered until polling day before both the parliamentary elections in 1995 and the presidential elections in 1996.[6] Claims of ballot falsification and more serious abuses increasingly have blemished the legitimacy of most votes in Russia at both the national and the regional levels.[7] Finally, violations of campaign finance laws, governmental monopoly of television time, and intimidation tactics by local executives indicate that there is still not a free and level playing field in the Russian political arena.

Elections in Russia have not produced outcomes typical of most democratic transitions around the world because Russia has undergone a protracted transition to democracy accompanied by a simultaneous change in the economy and the borders of the state. In this context of peaceful but revolutionary change, elections initially threatened elites from the Soviet ancien régime while providing opportunities for new political actors and organizations.[8] Over time, however, and especially after 1993, when the last major battle between the challengers and defenders of the Soviet ancien régime ended in favor of the new order, members of the old elite have adapted to the new rules of electoral politics and have learned how to use or abuse elections to stay in power. Just as the Soviet economic elite was first threatened by free prices and privatization but then learned how to benefit from the new economic rules of the game, Soviet political elites also learned how to use elections to maintain political power. While elections in Russia initially helped open up the process to new entrants, they later served to consolidate and close the ruling elite's grip on power.[9]

The consequences of this adaptation have been mixed. On the positive side, the fact that Soviet elites became accustomed to elections marked the end of violent confrontation between challengers and defenders of the Soviet order. Though a small number of challengers to the current system still remain at the margins, most strategic actors in Russian politics today accept the basic rules of the game, especially the holding of regular elections for all major political offices. This new condition in Russia may even meet Schumpeter's minimalist definition of a democratic system: "the institutional arrangement for arriving at political decisions in which individuals acquire the power to decide by means of a competitive struggle for the people's vote."[10] On the negative side, the co-optation of the old Soviet elite has come at a high cost to democratic consolidation, because old elites have brought with them old habits and attitudes from the Soviet era.[11] Electoral procedures, laws, and associations are manipulated not to serve the greater interest of democracy, but rather to maintain political power. The reconsolidation of members of the Soviet elite into Russian political life also has effectively crowded out new actors and political organizations, particularly new political parties. The result has been the emergence of a political system in which elections play a central role, but which still lacks other important features of a consolidated democracy. In the formulation of political scientist Larry Diamond, Russia meets the conditions of an "electoral democracy" but does not yet have the additional protections for political and civic pluralism that would make it a "liberal democracy."[12]

Ironically, as documented below, these changes in elite strategies regarding elections have been accompanied by stability in electoral preferences within society. For most of Russia's recent electoral history, the voters have been polarized into two camps for and against the old order. This polarization began to subside only after President Yeltsin's electoral victory in 1996.

THE 1989 ELECTIONS TO THE USSR CONGRESS OF PEOPLE'S DEPUTIES

Elections to the USSR Congress of People's Deputies in 1989 were the first semicompetitive elections in Soviet history. Unable to garner support for his reform ideas within the Communist Party, General Secretary Mikhail Gorbachev hoped to resurrect the soviets[13] as a set of state institutions that would take governing power away from the Party.[14]

One-third of the 2,225 seats in the Congress were allocated to social organizations, which included everything from the Communist Party of the Soviet Union (CPSU) to the Soviet Academy of Sciences.[15] The remaining seats, divided equally between districts determined by administrative-territorial divisions and districts determined by population, were in theory subject to being contested by multiple candidates. In practice, cumbersome electoral procedures made the nomination of challengers from outside the *nomenklatura* system virtually impossible. To be nominated, candidates had to receive endorsements from either a workers collective or a public meeting of at least 500 people. Even after nomination, district electoral committees could disqualify any candidate—a power they exercised against almost half of all candidates.[16]

Nonetheless, these elections constituted a direct threat to the CPSU elite, since only the Party's top 100 officials were elected through the social organization list. These elections brought new people into the Russian political process: an estimated 88 percent of successful candidates were elected for the first time.[17] Only nine out of thirty-two CPSU first secretaries won in contested races. Out of seventy-five secretaries running unopposed, six still lost because they failed to receive the required 50-percent threshold of support.[18] The failure of the CPSU *nomenklatura* was most impressive in Leningrad, where both the first and second secretaries, as well as the majority of other, lower-level Party officials, failed to win seats.

While local CPSU leaders were humiliated, their losses did not translate directly into gains for new political actors—or "democrats," as they were then labeled. Eighty-five percent of the members of the new Soviet legislature were members of the CPSU, while none were members of an alternative political party at the time of the elections. At this stage, polarization between democrats and communists—the logic of Russian elections for the next seven years—did not yet play an important role. Instead, the main cleavage was between the old *nomenklatura* and the reform communists.

THE 1990 ELECTIONS OF THE RUSSIAN CONGRESS OF PEOPLE'S DEPUTIES

The 1990 elections of Russia's Congress of People's Deputies were more democratic and more competitive than the elections to the Soviet Congress had been in the previous year.[19] All seats were filled in first-past-the-post elections in two kinds of electoral districts—one defined territorially (168 seats), the other by the number of voters (900 seats). If no candidate won 50 percent approval in the first round, a runoff between the top two finishers occurred two weeks later.

Technically, political parties did not compete in this election, as the noncommunist parties were just forming. Article 6 of the Soviet Constitution, which had guaranteed the Communist Party of the Soviet Union the leading role in Soviet society, was repealed in February 1990, only weeks before the vote, which did not give new political parties enough time to organize. In addition, the ballots printed for this election failed to identify the party affiliation of candidates.

Nonetheless, these elections stimulated an explosion of grassroots political activity throughout Russia.[20] The sheer number of seats being contested meant that a large segment of the Russian population was involved in the nomination and campaign process. In addition, each district contest had its own unique characteristics. In the end, however, the elections were contested by two main camps: the democrats and the communists.

The democrats—identified as such by both their friends and enemies—had begun to organize as a united political force well before the spring of 1990. In January 1990 they founded a new organization called Democratic Russia, which assumed primary responsibility for coordinating candidate recruitment and campaign activity for the nascent democratic movement. Anticommunism, anti-status quo, and even anti-Gorbachevism were the common themes of Democratic Russia's "ideology of opposition."[21] The articulation of concrete alternative programs was not necessary at this stage in Russia's transition.

The second main player in the 1990 elections was the Communist Party of the Soviet Union (CPSU), which had split between reformers, who competed actively, and conservatives, who chose not to orchestrate a national campaign. Gorbachev and his immediate circle incorrectly assumed that the republic-level soviets were not as important as the USSR Congress of Peoples Deputies, and many CPSU officials campaigned as challengers and opponents to the party of power.[22]

Compared with the 1989 election, the 1990 election was regarded as a tremendous victory for Russia's democrats, who won roughly one-third of the 1,061 seats in the Russian Congress.[23] Communists won about 40 percent of the seats, while centrists occupied the *boloto* (the swamp, in Russian parlance) in the middle. Democratic Russia fared best in large urban centers, performing especially well in Moscow, Leningrad, and the Ural cities, while the communists dominated rural electoral districts.

The 1990 vote was a referendum on the status quo. To a greater extent than any election discussed in this chapter, the 1990 elections served to open up the political process to new individuals and political forces. At that stage in Russia's political transformation, elections still served a liberalizing function. The 1990 election also stimulated the emergence of proto-party politics. Democratic Russia occupied center stage as a united front of those opposed to the old Soviet order. Organizationally and ideologically, Russian politics had become polarized into those supporting the old order and those supporting Democratic Russia; significant third parties had not yet emerged. The 1990 elections also represented a major setback to CPSU elites. Although the party of power still won a majority of seats, the momentum had definitely swung to the democratic opposition.

THE JUNE 1991 PRESIDENTIAL ELECTION

The Russian presidential campaign began immediately after the March 1991 referendum in which Russian voters supported the introduction of the office of the presidency.[24] Throughout this pivotal year, politics in Russia remained polarized, pitting Boris Yeltsin and Russia's democrats against Mikhail Gorbachev, the increasingly isolated Soviet president.[25]

Assuming that he could rely on the liberal, urban electorate, Yeltsin selected as his running mate Colonel Aleksandr Rutskoi, head of the new parliamentary faction Communists for Democracy. A decorated Afghan veteran, Rutskoi was also expected to help Yeltsin win the votes of nationalists, military men, and moderates from the CPSU.

Nikolai Ryzhkov, a former CPSU Politburo member and Soviet prime minister, represented the ancien régime; he was considered to be more conservative than his former ally and colleague Gorbachev. Four other candidates qualified for the presidential ballot. The Yeltsin team worried that each would draw particular subsets of voters away from their candidate, with Vladimir Zhirinovsky taking populists; Aman Tuleev, non-Russian voters; Albert Makashov, the military vote; and Vadim Bakatin, CPSU reformers.

In fact, Yeltsin won a first-round victory, capturing 59.7 percent of the popular vote, compared with 17.6 percent for Ryzhkov, a surprising 8.1 percent for Zhirinovsky, and smaller percentages for Tuleev (7.1 percent), Makashov (3.9 percent), and Bakatin (3.6 percent). The vote reflected the crescendo of popular support for a change in the status quo. The Communist Party leaders saw this vote as a threat to their interests, while challengers to the Soviet communist system recognized it as an opportunity to consolidate their new political power.

THE 1993 PARLIAMENTARY ELECTIONS AND THE CONSTITUTIONAL REFERENDUM

Monumental changes took place in Russia between the June 1991 presidential election and December 1993 parliamentary elections.

Now the leader of an independent country, Yeltsin launched a radical economic reform in January 1992 designed to transform the Soviet command economy into a market economy. Preoccupied with this huge undertaking, Yeltsin did not pursue fundamental political transformation as well, but opted to leave in place many institutions and leaders from the old order. He did not, for example, threaten deputies in the Russian Congress or local CPSU elites with a new round of elections. The Russian Congress of People's Deputies assumed the role of the parliament, and Yeltsin appointed several former CPSU first secretaries to the new positions of heads of administration in their regions.

The Congress of People's Deputies soon became the leading institution opposing Yeltsin's revolutionary agenda. With no formal or even informal institutions to structure relations between the president and the legislature, both Yeltsin and the Congress of People's Deputies claimed sovereign authority over Russian territory. The period of dual sovereignty ended in bloodshed in October 1993, when Yeltsin used military force to defeat his opponents in Congress.

Yeltsin's presidential decree No. 1400, issued on September 21, 1993, dissolved the Congress of People's Deputies and called for a referendum to adopt a new constitution, plus immediate elections for a new bicameral parliament. In the run-up to the December vote, it was clear that different political actors had radically different ideas about which of the forthcoming national ballots was most important.

For Yeltsin, the key vote was for the new constitution, since this new basic law granted extraordinary powers to the president's office and legitimated the shift in the balance of power between Yeltsin and his challengers that had occurred in October. Surprisingly, Yeltsin did nothing to influence the electoral campaigns for either house of parliament.

The upper house poll mattered most to the regional elites, as it offered them a mechanism to fortify their existing political power. The electoral regulations and short campaign period aided incumbents tremendously. Each *oblast*, republic, and *krai* constituted one electoral district with two mandates rather than two single-mandate districts. Since name recognition virtually assured a sitting head of administration at least a second place finish, this electoral system helped incumbents avoid defeat. The combination of a brief registration period and the need to obtain the signatures of 2 percent of the region's total population meant that, with few exceptions, only candidates supported by the local administration could get on the ballot.[26] In dozens of regions, three candidates made the ballot—two from the local administration and a third unknown candidate allowed to register simply to ensure that the electoral results were legitimate.

The vote for the State Duma, the lower house, was most important for Moscow elites and especially for Russia's democratic forces. Yeltsin's decree on elections stated that the lower house would be elected according to a mixed system: half the 450 seats would be determined by a majoritarian system in newly drawn electoral districts, while the other half would to be allocated according to a system of proportional representation (PR). Parties had to win at least 5 percent to win seats on the PR ballot.[27]

For the first time in Russia's electoral history, parties dominated the menu of electoral choices. On the reformist side, four electoral blocs once united in Democratic Russia qualified for the ballot: Russia's Choice, Yabloko, the Party of Russian Unity and Accord, and the Movement for Democratic Reform.[28] The leaders of these parties believed that reformists would win more seats running as separate blocs than as one party or organization. The communists, now considered the opposition, also split and ran as two entities: the Communist Party of the Russian Federation (CPRF, the main successor to the seventy-year-old CPSU) and the Agrarian Party of Russia (APR). Several centrist groups that asserted that Russia needed a set of third, moderate political forces to temper the polarized politics of democrat versus communist also earned places on the ballot, but only one nationalist party—Vladimir Zhirinovsky's Liberal Democratic Party of Russia—qualified for the PR ballot.

The results of the first two elections matched most observers' expectations. In the referendum, 58.4 percent of the voters supported Yeltsin's constitution while 41.2 percent were opposed. Turnout was reported to be 54.8 percent, which ensured that the referendum was valid. Some observers complained, however, that the Yeltsin administration had inflated the turnout and that the referendum on the constitution was not as free and fair as other elections had been.[29]

Elections to the Federation Council, the upper house, also produced few surprises. The range of competitive candidates appeared to be narrowing. Only eight of the sixty-six heads of administration who competed in these elections lost. Only a handful of candidates who were not affiliated with either the old or the new regional elites won. With few exceptions, successful candidates were members either of the Communist Party of the Russian Federation or of the ruling party of power. The two-mandate ballot also created opportunities for falsification. Unaccustomed to voting for more than one candidate, many voters marked only one name, giving local electoral commissioners an easy opportunity to mark a second name during ballot counting.

The results of the Duma elections, however, were shocking. More than any previous vote in Russia, this vote was dominated by new political forces. Leaders of several of the successful "reformist," "centrist," and "nationalist" blocs were not closely affiliated with the former Soviet *nomenklatura*. As expected, the PR vote did stimulate the formation of a party system at the national level in Russia. Quite unexpectedly, however, the final arrival of multiparty politics in Russia was initially dominated by an extremist nationalist party—Vladimir Zhirinovsky's LDPR.

The LDPR won almost a quarter of the popular vote. Russia's Choice secured a paltry 15 percent, or less than half of what had been expected, while the other democratic parties each won less than 10 percent of the popular vote. The Russian Communist Party and its rural comrades, the Agrarians, combined for less than 20 percent of the vote, while new centrist groups combined for nearly a quarter of the vote.

Elections for Duma single-mandate seats did not parallel the PR ballot. Successful candidates were predominantly from the old Soviet *nomenklatura*, although they made up a smaller percentage of victors in the Duma than in the Federation Council. Agrarian candidates won in rural areas; Communists dominated in the so-called red belt (Russia's poor rust belt region); and candidates supported by the local party of power prevailed in major urban areas. Outsiders—whether democrats, nationalists, neocommunists, or centrists—fared poorly. (Since party affiliation was not indicated on the ballot, parties did not play a significant role in single-mandate races.)

Compared with the referendum vote and the Federation Council elections, there was little evidence of fraud in the Duma elections. This may have reflected the Yeltsin administration's lack of concern about the composition of the lower house, since real power remained vested in the Kremlin. The president also was certain to have a loyal Federation Council.

Although Zhirinovsky had placed third in the 1991 presidential vote, he and his party had not been considered serious contenders in the 1993 vote. As late as mid-November, public opinion surveys gave Zhirinovsky's Liberal Democratic Party less than 2 percent of popular support. His sudden, dramatic surge in the final days of the campaign shocked everyone. Most interpretations of the 1993 elections focused on Zhirinovsky's phenomenal performance on the party ballot. With the advantage of hindsight, however, Zhirinovsky's 1993 victory does not appear to have marked the beginning of fascism's ascendance in Russia. After enduring two and half years of falling production, double-digit inflation, and general economic uncertainty, Russian voters were expected to follow their counterparts throughout Eastern Europe and to vote against those affiliated with the incumbent government. The key difference was that Russia's communists (unlike their counterparts in Eastern Europe) had not reorganized as social democratic parties but had continued to advocate a return to the past—a stance that helped precipitate the October 1993 standoff between President Yeltsin and the Congress of People's Deputies. In the immediate aftermath of the October 1993 confrontation, the communists were in disarray. Weeks before the December vote, it was uncertain whether members of the Russian Communist Party would even be allowed to participate. In contrast, Zhirinovsky's brilliant television campaign—the first real mass media campaign in Russian electoral history—established his party as the most aggressive and abrasive enemy of the status quo.[30] Finally, the PR electoral system itself helped account for Zhirinovsky's victory. Capturing almost a quarter of the popular vote on the party list, the LDPR won 57 seats in the Duma through the PR system.[31] In single-mandate races, however, LDPR candidates won only 5 seats in the Duma and no seats in the Federation Council. In a purely majoritarian electoral system, the Liberal Democratic Party would have won fewer than ten seats in the parliament.

Zhirinovsky's stellar campaign performance contrasted sharply with the abysmal effort of Russia's democrats, who had decided not to unite in a single bloc. The vote for democratic parties in the PR ballot was split, making the democratic defeat look worse than it really was. An electoral outcome in which a democratic coalition won 34 percent of the popular vote—the sum of the votes for Russia's Choice, Yabloko, the Party of Russian Unity and Accord, and the Russian Movement for Democratic Reforms—would have looked quite different from the December outcome, when the most popular party won only 15 percent.[32]

To make matters worse, democratic leaders Yegor Gaidar and Grigory Yavlinsky spent most of the campaign quarreling with each other instead of criticizing more serious opponents such as Zhirinovsky. In dozens of single-mandate races, multiple candidates from democratic parties split the vote, allowing both communists and nationalists to win seats with as little as 15 percent of the popular vote. Russia's Choice had no campaign strategy or effective organization. The bloc, which was founded only two months before the election, tried to fuse together federal and regional government elites with grassroots activists from the Democratic Russia Movement. But when Yeltsin refused to affiliate himself with Russia's Choice, the bloc was left with the uncharismatic and unpopular Gaidar as its leader. The absence of a strong and attractive leader was readily apparent in the bloc's poor electoral showing.

1995 PARLIAMENTARY ELECTIONS

The parliament elected in 1993 was an interim body whose term expired after two years. Preparations for the 1995 election began immediately after the conclusion of the 1993 balloting. For the first time in Russia's tumultuous democratic transition, a legitimate constitution was in place. While communists criticized the document for giving too much power to the president, they neither challenged its legitimacy nor engaged in extraconstitutional or illegal political practices.

A new law stipulated that the Federation Council would be composed of two officials from each subnational territory—the chairman of the legislature and the head of administration. Both of these officials had to be elected locally, a major advantage for regional elites, who could retain local power and gain a legislative voice in national affairs. It also meant that parties would have a marginal role in the upper house, since few *oblast* and *krai* governors or republican presidents publicly identified with a political party.

The rules for the 1995 parliamentary elections were similar to those organizing the 1993 vote, but with some important differences. The new law reaffirmed the basic structure of the Duma, despite attempts by Yeltsin's supporters to increase the number of single-mandate seats and to decrease the number of seats allocated according to proportional representation,[33] changes that would have impeded party development and increased disorganization within the Duma. The Yeltsin forces believed that deputies from single-mandate districts were more likely to be controlled by regional elites and more prone to cooperation with the Kremlin. In the end, however, the president and his administration abided by the new law.

The new law allowed candidates running in single-mandate districts to list their party affiliations on the ballot. And it mandated that parliamentary and presidential elections not occur simultaneously, ensuring that Yeltsin would not have to associate himself with any electoral bloc competing in the parliamentary vote.[34] With only six months before the next scheduled presidential election, many thought of the 1995 ballot as a primary for the bigger prize in 1996.[35]

The number of electoral blocs that registered for the ballot increased from thirteen in 1993 to forty-three in 1995. Eight of the new electoral blocs in 1995 were direct descendants of Russia's Choice from 1993, while as many as twenty blocs emerged from the Democratic Russia of 1991. Early in the campaign period, the Yeltsin administration openly promoted the formation of two new electoral blocs dominated by former CPSU *apparatchiks* who had switched allegiance to Yeltsin's consolidating party of power. Victor Chernomyrdin's Our Home Is Russia bloc was supposed to represent right-of-center forces, while Ivan Rybkin was ordered to form a left-of-center bloc.

The Kremlin's strategy changed when it became clear that the two parties initiated by the Yeltsin administration were not capable of winning a majority. Some months before the 1995 vote, the Yeltsin team began to stimulate party proliferation to impede the consolidation of Russia's reformist forces. Above all else, the president did not want a single party leader to emerge from the 1995 vote as the leader of the democrats, since Yeltsin himself planned to emerge as the focal point for the reformers in the presidential election.

Competition for the nationalist vote also increased as several new nationalist and patriotic groups appeared on the ballot in 1995, including, most importantly, the Congress of Russian Communities, headed by Yuri Skokov and General Aleksandr Lebed; Derzhava, led by former vice president Aleksandr Rutskoi; and Power to the People, headed by Sergei Baburin and former Soviet premier Nikolai Ryzhkov.

Between 1993 and 1995, the Communist Party had devoted tremendous energy and resources to rebuilding networks and structures left from decades of communist rule. In fact, the CPRF was

TABLE 1
Russian Parliamentary Elections, 1993 and 1995

Parties and Movements	1995 Elections				1993 Elections
	Party-List Seats	Single-Mandate Seats	Total Duma Seats	Percentage of Party-List Vote	Percentage of Party-List Vote
Reformist					
Our Home is Russia	45	10	55	10.3	—
Yabloko	31	14	45	7.0	7.9
Democratic Choice of Russia	0	9	9	3.9	15.5
Other/Independent	0	33	33	3.6	4.1
Total	**76**	**66**	**142**	**24.8**	**27.5**
Centrist					
Women of Russia	0	3	3	4.7	8.1
Worker's Self-Management	0	1	1	4.0	—
Other/Independent	0	38	38	2.6	15.4
Total	**0**	**42**	**42**	**11.3**	**23.5**
Opposition					
Communist Party	99	58	157	22.3	12.4
Liberal Democratic Party	50	1	51	11.2	22.9
Agrarians	0	20	20	3.8	8.0
Working Russia	0	1	1	4.5	—
Congress of Russian Communities	0	5	5	4.3	—
Other/Independent	0	31	31	5.2	0
Total	**149**	**116**	**265**	**51.3**	**43.3**

Sources: Bulletins of the Russian Central Election Commission, 1993 and 1995.
Note: Table includes all parties that received at least 3 percent of the party-list vote. The following reformist parties received between 1 and 3 percent of the vote: Forward Russia (2.0), Pamfilova-Gurov-Lysenko bloc (1.6), Ivan Rybkin's bloc (1.1). The following opposition parties received between 1 and 3 percent of the vote: Derzhava (2.6), Power to the People (1.6), Stanislav Govorukhin's bloc (1.0). Parties with less than 1 percent are not included in the two right-hand columns.

the largest and most organized party competing in the 1995 elections. Viktor Anpilov's radical Working Russia was the only major new electoral bloc to compete for the communist vote. The CPRF made impressive gains, winning almost a quarter of the popular vote, and reclaiming its role as the leader of the opposition. Buoyed by party identification on the ballot, CPRF candidates also dominated in single-mandate races, winning an astonishing 58 seats. Zhirinovsky won less than half his 1993 total, but still placed second with 11 percent of the popular vote. Viktor Chernomyrdin's Our Home Is Russia was the only reformist party to break through to double digits. The Yabloko party, led by Grigory Yavlinsky, the self-proclaimed leader of Russia's democratic opposition, won 7 percent— well below expectations and almost a full percentage point below Yabloko's 1993 showing. Former acting prime minister Yegor Gaidar and his Democratic Choice of Russia suffered the greatest setback in 1995, winning only 3.9 percent of the popular vote—or less than one-third of their 1993 total.

Most analysts interpreted these results as a victory for hard-line forces, a major setback for democratic parties, and a firm rebuff of both Yeltsin and Prime Minister Chernomyrdin.[36] When framed through a bipolar lens, however, the 1995 vote looked similar to previous elections. The Agrarians performed so poorly that they failed to cross the 5 percent threshold needed to win PR seats. The combination of a Communist surge, an Agrarian Party collapse, and Zhirinovsky's comparatively poorer showing meant that the total votes cast for opposition parties had changed only marginally in two years.

In the aggregate, there was the same stability of voter attitudes on the other side of the ledger. In 1993 Gaidar's Russia's Choice, Yavlinsky's Yabloko, and the now defunct Russian Movement for Democratic Reforms combined to win 28 percent of the popular vote. In 1995 Our Home Is Russia, Yabloko, and Russia's Choice together collected 21 percent of the vote, with an additional 7 percent of the vote divided among small reformist parties.

Two significant changes, however, did occur in 1995. The balance of support within these two broad camps of voters changed considerably. Leaders and parties from the old Soviet *nomenklatura* now dominated both the reformist and opposition wings of Russia's polarized political spectrum. New political actors with weak ties to the old Soviet elite on both sides—whether Zhirinovsky, Yavlinsky, or Gaidar—had been pushed even further to the margins.

There was also a collapse of electoral support for apolitical, ideologically vague, centrist parties and blocs. Whereas these kinds of parties and personalities won almost a quarter of the popular vote on the party list ballot, and approximately a third of the single mandate seats in 1993, they were obliterated in 1995 on both ballots. Once again, Russian politics looked increasingly bipolar.

On the whole, all major political actors accepted the election results as valid. Pockets of ballot falsification, including massive irregularities in Chechnya, were reported, but these tainted the electoral results only at the margins. Our Home Is Russia also violated spending limits and dominated the national television airwaves. Given the relative impotence of the Duma in governing Russia, the stakes in this election were rather low.

1996 PRESIDENTIAL ELECTION

The 1995 parliamentary election did serve, however, as a primary for the vitally important election of the president in the summer of 1996.[37] The results established Communist Party leader Gennady Zyuganov as the leading candidate of the opposition, but were much less conclusive on the reformist side. Neither Chernomyrdin, nor Yavlinsky, nor even Lebed emerged from the parliamentary vote as the undisputed leader. This left Yeltsin able to claim to be the only candidate capable of defeating Zyuganov, who seemed increasingly likely to advance to the second round. By March 1996 polls unambiguously showed that Yeltsin had captured that core reformist vote. To win in the second round, then, both Yeltsin and Zyuganov had to reach beyond their core supporters to centrist voters with amorphous political views.

Yeltsin's strategy was simple: to convince these voters that he was the lesser of two evils and that severe revolutionary turmoil would follow a Zyuganov victory. First, Yeltsin's image had to be changed. The president lost twenty pounds, stopped drinking, and began to appear frequently in public. Second, negative policies had to be changed. Public opinion polls demonstrated that two were most salient—unpaid wages and the war in Chechnya.[38] To create a sense of urgency around the issue, Yeltsin formed a special government commission tasked with paying all salaries by April. He also sacked a number of regional heads of administration as well as several of his own cabinet officials, including Anatoly Chubais, the deputy prime minister.[39] Yeltsin raised pensions, increased salaries of government employees (including military personnel), began doling out government transfers, and pledged at the end of March to end the war in Chechnya. In May the first Russian troops began to leave the embattled province. The president's team also unleashed a hard-hitting negative media blitz, successfully defining the election as a referendum on seventy years of Soviet communism—not one on Yeltsin's record.[40]

The last component of Yeltsin's campaign strategy was a March 1996 pact with General Aleksandr Lebed. Lebed agreed to join Yeltsin's government between the first and second rounds of the presidential election. In return, Yeltsin's financial allies got the green light to support Lebed's presidential campaign and Lebed was allowed to appear in mass media outlets controlled by Yeltsin. The Lebed deal also prevented a possible alliance between presidential hopefuls Lebed, Yavlinsky, and Svyatoslav Fyodorov.

Zyuganov started his presidential campaign in a much stronger position than Yeltsin, with 25 percent of the population already effectively pledged to vote for him in January—a time when Yeltsin's popular support was only in the single digits. The communist challenger and his campaign team understood that to win a majority of votes in the second round, they had to capture a segment of the so-called centrist vote.[41] But they erroneously believed that Russia's political spectrum consisted of three parts—democrats, communists, and nationalists. To reach beyond his core communist supporters, Zyuganov championed nationalist and patriotic themes rather than economic issues or social-democratic slogans.[42] It appears that this strategy succeeded, at least partially, because Zyuganov received more support in the second round than communist parties had won in previous elections. But his nationalist rhetoric also frightened away centrist voters who were tired of confrontational politics and longed for stability.

The CPRF's organizational capacity to run a grassroots, door-to-door campaign was extremely effective in mobilizing loyal communist supporters, but less effective in reaching new, undecided voters, especially those who typically received political information through television. The Party had limited financial resources, limited access to Russia's pro-Yeltsin television networks, and no experience in using television for campaign purposes. In the second round, centrist voters went overwhelmingly for Boris Yeltsin, who captured 54 percent of the popular vote, compared with 40 percent for Zyuganov. In contrast to the electoral history of most of postcommunist Europe, Russian voters opted to retain their first democratically elected leader for a second term.

The 1996 presidential election was marred by several irregularities. The Yeltsin forces enjoyed total control of the national television airwaves: every nightly news program reported favorably and often on the Yeltsin campaign while ignoring or airing negative reports about other candidates. Backed by every major financial and industrial group in the country, the Yeltsin team accumulated an almost limitless war chest and grossly violated the legal campaign spending limits. There were also scattered reports of ballot falsification throughout Russia, especially in the national republics, where vote swings away from Zyuganov between rounds were dramatic. In Tatarstan, for example, Zyuganov won fewer votes in the two-candidate second round than he did in the multicandidate first round (a most improbable outcome in the absence of fraud).

Finally, throughout the entire campaign period, Yeltsin government officials openly advocated the postponement of the vote altogether. While Yeltsin ultimately abided by the electoral process and fired the advocates of postponement from his administration, the specter of postponement cast a long, undemocratic shadow over the electoral process. Some communist campaign officials asserted that Zyuganov essentially gave up toward the end of the race, believing that he had no chance of winning power.

The 1996 presidential vote reaffirmed Russia's divided and polarized electorate. A majority once again opted for reform over regress, and the balance of support for both positions had not changed appreciably over previous binary votes.

The 1996 presidential vote also underscored the ancillary role played by political parties in determining electoral outcomes. Two of the top three candidates—Yeltsin and Lebed—ran without a party affiliation. Even Zyuganov, who ran as the Communist Party candidate, tried to distance his campaign from his party by creating the National Patriotic Bloc. Finally, the electoral process in 1996 looked less democratic than earlier votes in Russia, raising questions about whether the incumbent regime was a positive or a negative force with respect to further democratic consolidation.

THE 1996 GUBERNATORIAL ELECTIONS

The atmosphere of intense polarization and heightened confrontation present during the 1996 presidential campaign virtually disappeared after the election. Zyuganov and his party accepted defeat, participated in Yeltsin's inauguration, and overwhelmingly approved Victor Chernomyrdin as Yeltsin's choice for prime minister. Zyuganov then announced the formation of a new political organization, the National Patriotic Union of Russia (NPSR), which he asserted would be more moderate, centrist, and nationalist than the CPRF. Above all, Zyuganov proclaimed that his new political organization supported the current system and that it had no intention of undermining the current regime. The NPSR announced plans to support a dozen candidates in the coming cycle of fifty-two gubernatorial elections, but the new organization specifically avoided backing extremist challengers—even when this meant not supporting the favorites of more radical local Communist Party officials.

Suddenly, the main cleavage in Russian politics was no longer between communist and anticommunist world views. The gubernatorial elections were virtually devoid of ideology, political platforms, or national issues.[43] Instead, competence, name recognition, and relations with the Kremlin emerged as factors that decided electoral outcomes. With few exceptions, these gubernatorial races were still contests between an incumbent loyal to Yeltsin and a communist challenger, but the differences separating such candidates became increasingly difficult to recognize. While incumbents lost in about half of the fifty races scheduled in the fall of 1996, this large turnover did not appear to produce a major ideological reorientation of Russia's governors as a group. Moreover, so-called radical or extreme candidates who did win, such as former vice president Aleksandr Rutskoi, signaled their eagerness to cooperate with Yeltsin's government soon after taking power.[44] Beyond Zyuganov's new coalition and Yeltsin's party of power, other political parties played only marginal roles in all but a handful of these gubernatorial races.

Similarly, new political groups and parties independent of the new party of power and the old party of power (the communists) played only a marginal role in local legislative elections. In most regions, executives at the city and district levels, or representatives loyal to the regional heads of government, constituted the majority in these local dumas.

TRACING ELECTORAL TRENDS

For the first seven years of competitive elections in Russia, candidates and voters were divided between those who defended the old Soviet order and those who opposed it. This is extraordinary in two respects. In most successful transitions from communist rule to democracy, the communist–anticommunist divide no longer remained significant after the first election. In Russia, this divide continued to shape electoral contests several years after the collapse of Soviet communism in 1991. It is also extraordinary how stable the balance of support between the two camps remained during this period. Most amazingly, Boris Yeltsin won 54 percent of the vote in 1996—only 6 percent less than he won in his first presidential race in 1991. Elsewhere (in Central Europe, for example), electoral preferences have generally shifted from overwhelming support for anti-communists in the first free elections, to support for social-democratic or communist challengers in the next elections, and then back to those originally affiliated with the democratic revolution in the third round. The stability in Russian electoral preferences is especially striking when contrasted with the tremendous socio-economic and political changes that unfolded in the country during the same period.

But the stable polarization has been prolonged principally by the lack of agreement among Russian elites on the post-Soviet political and economic rules of the game. Yeltsin's victory over his opponents in the fall of 1993—his second such victory in as many years—shifted the balance of power in favor of the new order. The ratification of the new constitution soon thereafter helped consolidate this new order. Nonetheless, Zyuganov's Communist Party still did not look like it was totally committed to the existing regime throughout the 1996 presidential campaign.[45] Only after Zyuagnov's electoral defeat in 1996 did the divide between the communist and anticommunist forces begin to subside.

The withering away of this divide should fundamentally change electoral politics in Russia in the future. As demonstrated in gubernatorial races in the fall of 1996, a campaign strategy that promises to prevent a communist restoration will no longer work. Likewise, Communist Party candidates can no longer rely on nostalgia for the Soviet past to win votes. The collapse of this previously hegemonic cleavage issue will create room for new issues and ideas—particularly economic ones—to shape electoral preferences.[46] Voters also will be able to reject poorly performing incumbents without worrying that a change in power might result in new revolutionary struggle. The battle between communism and capitalism is over.

Changes in Elite Attitudes Toward Elections

If the Russian electorate has demonstrated a consistent set of attitudes throughout recent electoral history, Russia's elites have not. The political function of elections, in fact, has changed considerably between 1989 and 1996. Gorbachev initiated elections in 1989 to fortify his own position. As it happened, elections in 1989, 1990, and 1991 allowed political actors and organizations not affiliated with the CPSU *nomenklatura* to assume central political roles for the first time in seventy years, representing a direct threat to Soviet political elites.

After the collapse of the Soviet Union, however, elections increasingly served to consolidate power for those already in office. By 1996 almost all elected officials in positions of real power—whether from Yeltsin's party of power or from Gennady Zyuganov's CPRF— were members of the former CPSU elites. The only elections not dominated by these old elites were to political institutions that had only marginal power. Thus, elections to the Duma in 1993 and in 1995 looked more democratic and competitive than other elections precisely because the Duma was generally regarded as less powerful than the presidency or the Federation Council.

Party Stagnation

The changing function of elections in Russia has stunted the development of grassroots political parties and of a true multiparty system. Russian politics is now dominated by two parties of power rather than one. To be sure, the fact that elections are competitive and incumbents can lose power through the ballot box represents real progress compared with the communist past. Nonetheless, both the party of power and the communists emerged from the CPSU *nomenklatura*. Increasingly, and especially since the 1996 presidential vote, the differences between these two groups have become less obvious. Both accept the new political and economic order in Russia; both wish to maintain or gain a stake in executive governance at all levels of government; and both fear challengers to the status quo—whether populists like General Lebed, neocommunists like Viktor Anpilov, or grassroots democrats like Grigory Yavlinsky.

The consolidation of these former Soviet elites within Russia's superpresidential system has left little room for ideological definition or political party formation.[47] Yavlinsky's Yabloko, Zhirinovsky's LDPR, and Aleksandr Lebed's new Russian People's Republican Party represent potential challengers to Russia's two-party system, but the future of all of these new parties is still uncertain. Their inability to compete in the 1996 gubernatorial elections on a national basis suggests that the newcomers are still in the early stages of party development.

Freer and Fairer?

There have been some real achievements since the highly controlled Russian elections in 1989. First, the rules governing the electoral process have been codified as laws. If Gorbachev in 1989 and Yeltsin in 1993 could dictate the rules of the electoral game through the power of decree, neither Yeltsin nor any other governmental official can wield such discretionary authority concerning elections now.

Second, the nomination process has become less complicated, making it increasingly difficult for election commissions to disqualify candidates. During the parliamentary elections in 1995, for example, the Central Electoral Commission tried to disqualify two major electoral blocs—Yabloko and Derzhava—for minor technical infractions. In 1989, the CEC decision would have prevailed; in 1995, it did not, and both blocs appeared on the ballot.

Third, after hitting a democratic nadir in 1993 by refusing to publish the complete election results, the Central Electoral Commission has become increasingly transparent in its counting procedures. Independent election monitors still have no authority to watch election counts, but party representatives can and do. And after both the 1995 and 1996 elections, the commission published the full results.

Fourth, the number of candidates participating in elections appears to be growing. In 1989 there was an average of two candidates per seat. In 1990 this average rose to 6.3 in the Russian Congress elections; 6 in the 1991 presidential elections; 7 in 1993 Duma elections; 11.7 in the 1995 Duma vote; and 10 in the 1996 presidential race.

At the same time, there have been several serious negative trends. Executive incumbents have gained greater control over media outlets at both the federal and the regional levels. The growing importance of money in campaigns has also made the electoral process less competitive and more prone to corruption. Despite an increase in the number of candidates participating, the intensity of competition appears to be decreasing, as the average winner's margin over the second-place finisher has increased from 9.9 percent in 1993 to 12.7 percent in 1995 and to 13.5 percent in 1996. Finally, repeated instances of ballot falsification have gone unpunished, demonstrating a growing weakness of societal control over state actions.

CONCLUSION

Many observers, including most of the grassroots leaders of Russia's democratic movement of the late 1980s and early 1990s, have concluded that the transition to democracy in Russia has failed. In their view, several years after the fall of communism, Russia still has no truly democratic parties, no democratic procedures, and no democrats. As Lev Ponomarev, one of the cochairs of Democratic Russia remarked during the 1996 presidential race, it is better to have as president a "liberal" communist (Yeltsin) than a "conservative" communist (Zyuganov), but ultimately they are both still communists. Similarly, General Lebed lamented in an interview in February 1997 that, "Superficially, it appears that Russia has two elites, a communist elite and a democratic elite, but under the surface they are one and the same. . . . As a result, nothing can be changed here as long as those people remain in power."[48]

The success of these old elites in reacquiring political power, especially executive power, and the absence of new democratic organizations raises serious questions about the prospects for liberal democracy in Russia. While few would question that the Soviet command economy has been replaced by a Russian market economy (however flawed), many still question whether Russia has succeeded in replacing Soviet autocratic political institutions with genuine democratic practices. Can a real transformation of the political system have taken place if the same people who ruled under the ancien régime are still in power today?

Our answer is a cautious yes. While the actors may have remained the same, they now play by quite different rules. The very acceptance of elections by all strategic actors as the only legitimate method of assuming political power has served to institutionalize an important component of Russia's nascent democracy.[49] Russia still needs to perfect many essential attributes of liberal democracy, including competitive political parties, a vibrant civil society, the rule of law, and a free press.[50] At the same time, by establishing elections as the only game in town, Russia's new political system has made a fundamental break with its totalitarian past.

In the near future, elections may continue to consolidate the political power of elites from the Soviet era. Just as insider or *nomenklatura* privatization marks the new economic system, the contemporary beneficiaries of the new political system so far are the very elites that originally opposed democratic reform. In the long run, however, the recurrence of elections will establish the institutional context for future challenges to the status quo. Especially now that the polarized struggle between communism and capitalism is over, Russian voters can be expected to be less tolerant of the shortcomings of their current leadership in the next round of national elections. The current ruling elite's failure to deliver on even basic commitments to voters will create opportunities for outsiders and new political parties. As long as the electoral process remains in place, even a coalition of the new party of power with the old party of power would not be able to maintain its dominance indefinitely. Russia's democratic consolidation—though delayed by several years—may soon begin to follow the patterns observed in other postcommunist countries. Although the results of recent Russian elections may not have produced immediate stimulants for further political reform, both the process and the repetition of elections have provided an enabling institutional context for reform initiatives in the future.

NOTES

[1] The Russian Federation is made up of twenty-one republics (*respubliki*), six territories (*kraia*), forty-nine regions (*oblasti*), one Jewish autonomous region (*avtonomnaya oblast*), ten autonomous areas (*avtonomnie okruga*), and two "cities of federal importance," Moscow and St. Petersburg.

[2] For elaboration on this comparison, see Michael McFaul, "Lessons from Russia's Protracted Transition from Communist Rule," *Political Science Quarterly*, vol. 114, no. 1 (1999), pp. 1–28.

[3] Guillermo O'Donnell and Philippe Schmitter, eds., *Transitions from Authoritarian Rule: Tentative Conclusions about Uncertain Democracies* (Baltimore: Johns Hopkins University Press, 1986).

[4] This learning period takes longer in postcommunist transitions, as the traditional class-based identities in society are also in flux. On the questionable relationship between social structure and party development in the postcommunist world, see Herbert Kitschelt, "The Formation of Party Systems in East Central Europe," *Politics and Society*, vol. 20, no.1 (1992), pp. 7–50; Valerie Bunce and Maria Csanadi, "Uncertainty in the Transition: Post-Communism in Hungary," *East European Politics and Society*, vol. 7 (1993), pp. 240–75; Geoffrey Evans and Stephen Whitefield, "Identifying the Bases of Party Competition in Eastern Europe," *British Journal of Political Science*, vol. 23, no. 4 (1993), pp. 521–48; and M. Steven Fish, "The Advent of Multipartism in Russia, 1993–1995," *Post-Soviet Affairs*, vol. 11, no. 4 (October–December 1995), pp. 340–83.

[5] VTsIOM (All-Russian Center for the Study of Public Opinion), "Pyat' Let Reforma," mimeo, 1996.

[6] David Remnick, "The War for the Kremlin," *New Yorker*, July 22, 1996.

[7] Farcical elections, such as the vote in Chechnya in December 1995; tragic violations of voters' rights, such as the ouster of an elected president in Mordovia in 1993, the removal of elected mayors in Vladivostok in 1994, in Ryazan in 1996, and in Izhevsk in 1996; and republican presidential elections with only one candidate in Ingushetiya (1993), Kalmykiya (1995), Tatarstan (1991 and 1996), and Kabardino-Balkaria (1996) all suggest that Russia's electoral procedures have not improved since the first semifree and quasi-fair elections in 1989.

[8] See Michael McFaul, "Revolutionary Transformation in Comparative Perspective: Defining a Post-Communist Research Agenda," in David Holloway and Norman Naimark, eds., *Reexamining the Soviet Experience: Essays in Honor of Alexander Dallin* (Boulder, Colo.: Westview Press, 1996), pp. 167–98.

[9] Drawing on the metaphor of the French revolution, some have called this latest stage the Thermidor. Compared with the English

revolution, this latest stage looks similar to the rapprochement between Tory and Whig elites in the Glorious Revolution of 1688–1689. In several respects, the English case is more akin to the Russian experience than the French one, since the formal rules of the game (that is, elections) were not abandoned or changed during consolidation or restoration. Instead, the function that these rules serve has been altered. See Crane Brinton, *The Anatomy of Revolution* (New York: Random House, 1938).

[10] Joseph Schumpeter, *Capitalism, Socialism, and Democracy* (New York: Harper, 1947), second edition, p. 269. For a more precise definition of the minimalist spirit invoked here, see the appendix to Adam Przeworski, Michael Alvarez, Jose Antonio Cheibub, and Fernando Limongi, "What Makes Democracy Endure?" in Larry Diamond, Marc Plattner, Yun-han Chu, and Hung-mao Tien, eds., *Consolidating the Third Wave Democracies: Themes and Perspectives* (Baltimore: Johns Hopkins University Press, 1997), pp. 306–8.

[11] Even during periods of revolutionary change, when new rulers make a conscious attempt to break with the past, the path of transformation is still shaped by the prior set of formal and informal institutions and practices. See Douglas North, *Institutions, Institutional Change, and Economic Performance* (Cambridge, UK: Cambridge University Press, 1990), p. 6; James G. March and Johan P. Olsen, *Rediscovering Institutions: The Organizational Basis of Politics* (New York: Free Press, 1989), pp. 64–5. Specific to the postcommunist world, see Kenneth Jowitt, *The New World Disorder: The Leninist Extinction* (Berkeley: University of California Press, 1992).

[12] See Diamond's essay, "Is the Third Wave Over?" *Journal of Democracy*, vol. 7, no. 3 (July 1996), pp. 20–37; see his *Developing Democracy: Towards Consolidation* (Baltimore: Johns Hopkins University Press, 1999), pp. 10–1, for additional attributes of liberal democracy that follow from this definition.

[13] Soviets were the parliamentary councils that rubberstamped Communist Party decisions for most of the Soviet era.

[14] Anatoly Sobchak, *Khozhdenie vo Vlast'* (Moscow: Novosti Publishers, 1991).

[15] Some of these social organizations' seats were contested internally, including the famous battle for Andrei Sakharov's election within the Soviet Academy of Sciences, in which a group of scientists

forced the Academy to put Sakharov on the ballot. The CPSU list, however, was not competitive. After considering competitive elections within the Party, Gorbachev opted for the nomination of exactly one hundred candidates to ensure that the Party leadership received seats in the Congress. See Georgi Shakhnazarov, *Tsena Svobody* (Moscow: Rossika-Zevs, 1993), pp. 74–5.

[16] See V. A. Kolosov, N. V. Petrov, and L. V. Smirnyagin, eds., *Vesna 89: Geografiya i Anatomiya Parlamentskikh Vyborov* (Moscow: Progress Publishers 1990).

[17] Stephen White, Richard Rose, Ian McAllister, *How Russia Votes* (Chatham, N.J.: Chatham House Publishers, 1997), p. 29. Elections, of course, occurred throughout most of Soviet history but had no real meaning.

[18] For details, see Michael McFaul and Nikolai Petrov, eds., *Politicheskii Al'manakh Rossii 1997*, (Moscow: Carnegie Moscow Center, 1998).

[19] Surprisingly little has been written in either Russia or the West on these pivotal elections. For a detailed study of the 1990 Moscow election, see Timothy Colton, "The Politics of Democratization: The Moscow Election of 1990," *Soviet Economy*, vol. 6, no. 4 (October–December 1990), pp. 285–344.

[20] For accounts, see M. Steven Fish, *Democracy from Scratch* (Princeton: Princeton University Press, 1993); and Geoffrey Hosking, *The Awakening of the Soviet Union* (Cambridge, Mass.: Harvard University Press, 1991).

[21] See Sergei Stankevich and Mikhail Schneider, *Rekomendatsii po taktike Kandidatov Demokraticheskogo Bloka i Ikh Kampanii, 1989–90 g.g.* (Moscow: Informtsentr Moskovskogo Narodnogo Fronta, 1990).

[22] Many democrats also underestimated the importance of this Russian-level election and did not participate. At the time, the Russian Federation had little to no autonomy from the Soviet state.

[23] Authors' interview in February 1997 with Vladimir Bokser, one of the campaign organizers for Democratic Russia in this election. The number of deputies who identified with Democratic Russia changed over time, depending on the nature of the crisis. See Thomas Remington, Steven Smith, Roderick Kiewiet, and Moshe Haspel, "Transitional Institutions and Parliamentary Alignments in Russia, 1990–1993," and Alexander Sobyanin, "Political Cleavages Among the Russian Deputies," both in Thomas Remington,

ed., *Parliaments in Transition: The New Legislative Politics in the Former USSR and Eastern Europe* (Boulder, Colo.: Westview Press, 1994).

24 For a detailed account of the 1991 campaign, see Michael Urban, "Boris El'tsin, Democratic Russia and the Campaign for the Russian Presidency," *Soviet Studies*, vol. 44, no. 2 (1992) pp. 187–207.

25 The best chronology of this period is John Dunlop, *The Rise of Russia and the Fall of the Soviet Empire* (Princeton: Princeton University Press, 1993).

26 At the same time that Yeltsin dissolved the Russian Congress of People's Deputies, dozens of local soviets were also disbanded. As the chairs of these local legislatures were generally also the leading opposition figures, the dissolutions stripped important organizational and institutional campaign resources from the potential challengers of local executive authorities only weeks before the 1993 vote.

27 For elaboration, see Robert Moser, "The Impact of the Electoral System on Post-Communist Party Development: The Case of the 1993 Russian Parliamentary Elections," *Electoral Studies*, vol. 14, no. 4 (1995), pp. 377–98.

28 Nikolai Travkin's Democratic Party of Russia was also a member of Democratic Russia, though the relationship between the two organizations had been difficult from the beginning.

29 A. A. Sobyanin, V. G. Sukhovolskii, *Demokratiya, Ogranichennaya Falsifikatsiyami: vybory i referendumy v Rossii v 1991–1993 gg.* (Moscow: Project Group on Human Rights, 1995).

30 Zhirinovsky appeared on television more often than any other electoral bloc leader. See *Russian Media Coverage of the Campaign* (Moscow: Russian-American Press and Information Center, December 15, 1993).

31 *Rossiiskaya gazeta*, December 28, 1993, pp. 2–3.

32 Regarding parliamentary seats, the democrats would have acquired an additional ten or eleven seats had Russian Movement for Democratic Reforms and its 4 percent of the popular vote been part of one of the proreform parties that did exceed the 5 percent threshold.

33 See the excellent article by Thomas Remington and Steven Smith, "Political Goals, Institutional Context, and the Choice of an Electoral System: The Russian Parliamentary Election Law," *American*

Journal of Political Science, vol. 40, no. 4, November 1996, pp. 1253–79.

[34] On the importance of electoral cycles, see Matthew Shugart and John Carey, *Presidents and Assemblies*, (Cambridge, UK: Cambridge University Press, 1992), chapter 9.

[35] For detailed accounts of the 1995 vote, see Michael McFaul, *Russia Between Elections: What the 1995 Parliamentary Elections Really Mean* (Washington, D.C.: Carnegie Endowment for International Peace, 1996); and Nikolai Petrov, ed., *Parlamentskie vybory 1995 goda v Rossii* (Moscow: Carnegie Moscow Center, 1996).

[36] See Peter Reddaway, "Red Alert," *New Republic*, January 29, 1996; Jerry Hough, Evelyn Davidheiser, and Susan Goodrich Lehman, *The 1996 Russian Presidential Election*, Brookings Occasional Papers (Washington, D.C.: Brookings Institution, 1996); Peter Stavrakis, "Russia After the Elections: Democracy or Parliamentary Byzantium?" *Problems of Post-Communism* (March–April 1996), pp. 13–20.

[37] For details, see Michael McFaul, *The Russian 1996 Presidential Election: The End of Polarized Politics* (Stanford: Hoover Institution Press, 1997).

[38] Fond "Obshchestvennoe mnenie", "Klyuchevye problemy predvybornoi kampanii v zerkale obshchestvennogo mneniya," *Rezultaty sotsiologicheskikh issledovanii*, no. 29, May 10, 1996, pp. 4–5.

[39] In late March, Chubais nonetheless returned to the Yeltsin team to run the campaign.

[40] See Aleksei Mukhin, Andrei Zapeklyi, and Nikita Tyukov, *Rossiya: Prezidentskaya Kampaniya–1996* (Moscow: SPIK-Tsentr, 1996).

[41] See the interview with Valentin Kuptsov, Zyuganov's campaign manager, in *Vek*, June 14, 1996, p. 5.

[42] See especially Gennady Zyuganov, speech before the Fourth Party Conference, February 15, 1996, reprinted in *Informatsionnyi byulleten'* (CPRF) no. 2 (35) February 20, 1996; and Zyuganov's campaign platform, *Rossiya, Rodina, Narod! Predvybornaya platforma kandidata na post prezidenta rossiiskoi federatsii G. A. Zyuganova*, reprinted in *Zavtra*, no. 12, 1996, p. 3.

[43] For details, see Michael McFaul and Nikolai Petrov, "Russian Electoral Politics After Transition: Regional and National Assessments," *Post-Soviet Geography and Economics*, vol. XXXVIII, no. 9 (November 1997), pp. 507–49.

[44] Rutskoi was the most dramatic example. In the fall of 1993, he spearheaded the defense of the Congress against Yeltsin and eventually called for a military overthrow of the Yeltsin regime. Upon his election as governor of Kursk in the fall of 1996, however, Rutskoi renounced his party leadership in the nationalist group Derzhava, which he had helped to found, and quickly traveled to Moscow to establish cooperative relations with his former enemies in the Kremlin.

[45] In contrast, former communist parties in Eastern Europe abandoned their commitment to the ancien régime and became social democratic parties almost immediately after the first election. See Michael Waller, "Party Inheritances and Party Identities," in Geoffrey Pridham and Paul Lewis, eds., *Stabilising Fragile Democracies: Comparing New Party Systems in Southern and Eastern Europe* (London: Routledge, 1996), pp. 23–43.

[46] Timothy Colton, "Economics and Voting in Russia," *Post-Soviet Affairs*, vol. 12, no. 4 (October–December 1996), especially pp. 314–5. Much of the literature on voting in the United States focuses on the role of economic variables, both at the individual and national levels. See, for example, Morris Fiorina, *Retrospective Voting in American National Elections* (New Haven: Yale University Press, 1981); Michael MacKuen, Robert Erikson, and James Stimson, "Peasants or Bankers? The American Electorate and the U.S. Economy," *American Political Science Review*, vol. 86, no. 3 (September 1992), pp. 597–611; Roderick Kiewet, *Macreconomics and Micropolitics* (Chicago: Chicago University Press, 1983); and Alberto Alesina, "Elections, Party Structure, and the Economy," in Jeffrey Banks and Eric Hanushek, eds., *Modern Political Economy* (Cambridge, UK: Cambridge University Press, 1995), pp. 145–70.

[47] On the negative influence of presidential systems on party development, see Juan Linz, "Presidential or Parliamentary Democracy: Does It Make A Difference?" in Juan Linz and Arturo Valenzuela, eds., *The Failure of Presidential Democracy, Vol. 1: Comparative Perspectives,* (Baltimore: Johns Hopkins University Press, 1994).

[48] Interview with Aleksandr Lebed by Pilar Bonet, *El Pais*, February 3, 1997.

[49] Adam Przeworski, "Democracy as a Contingent Outcome of Conflicts," in Jon Elster and Rune Slagstad, eds., *Constitutionalism and Democracy* (Cambridge, UK: Cambridge University Press, 1993), pp. 59–80.

[50] These deficiencies are explored in Michael McFaul, "Russia: Transition without Consolidation," *Freedom Review*, vol. 28, no. 1 (January 1997), pp. 38–57.

3
From Ethnos to Demos: the Quest for Russia's Identity

Valery Tishkov and Martha Brill Olcott

Throughout the decades of Soviet rule, the state tried to tell most people both who they were and what they should believe. In today's Russia, individuals are free to determine these things for themselves. But in trying to do so, ordinary citizens, as well as those charged with formulating official policy, confront a basic contradiction of the communist heritage. The Soviet Union declared itself to be an internationalist state based on class solidarity and social homogeneity—but it remained a state in which ethnic affiliation, expressed as nationality, was omnipresent and untransformable.

Soviet scholarship was long dominated by the need to legitimate the existing political divisions of the Soviet Union as natural ones. Its conceptions of ethnicity were based on Stalin's original categorization of Soviet society as consisting of nations, national communities, and peoples. While nationalists were persecuted and nationalism was considered one of the most serious political threats to the internationalist nature of the state, institutionalized and officially sponsored ethnic divisions nevertheless dominated Soviet society. The Communist Party developed an elaborate nationalities policy to monitor and manage the multicultural society under its control. The success of this policy in eliminating ethnic problems was considered an important achievement of the socialist system, which had failed to demonstrate its superiority in other areas, such as politics or the economy.

Maintaining a facade of ethnic equality became a mainstay of the Soviet regime. To this end, autonomous ethnic regions were proclaimed, and special educational and social welfare benefits were extended to them. At the same time, ethnic minorities were required to conform to the economic and political dictates of the local *nomenklatura* and of Communist Party leaders in Moscow. By the 1980s, it was quite clear that despite the numerous official efforts to propagate the idea of a single Soviet people, these ethnic boundaries and identities were far from being replaced by a sense of Soviet patriotism.[1] This was especially true for those ethnic communities with ties to nationalized homelands, that is, those with union or autonomous republics that bore their names.

Over time, the phrase "nationalities policy" came to be synonymous with the goal of managing the USSR's ethnic minorities and keeping watch over Russian nationalists. While Soviet policy makers argued over how much autonomy to allow the various ethnic communities, Soviet scholars were busy searching for ways to use such tools as school curriculum, language of instruction, and the mass media to reshape distinct ethnic communities into a single multinational people.

The intellectual foundation for this effort was a Soviet theory that held that all of human society was divided into archetypal ethnic communities, or *ethnoses*.[2] Ethnic communities varied considerably from one another throughout history, and these differences had been a common source of human conflict. Only under socialism, the theory held, could different ethnoses live in conditions of mutual respect and solidarity. By the early 1980s, the scope of nationalities policy had been extended to include such issues as the relationship of language usage and adherence to religious or other presocialist cultural values to linkages between economic development and the formation of Soviet patriotism.

During the Gorbachev years, non-Russian ethnic communities across the USSR began developing movements of national revival, even mass-supported independence movements. Russian nationalist forces—some with democratic and others with autocratic goals—were also emerging.[3] The growing influence of these movements contributed significantly to the speed with which the USSR collapsed, stimulated the emergence of new states, and later fueled intrastate and interstate conflicts in Armenia, Azerbaijan, Georgia, Moldova, and Russia itself.

The breakup of the USSR left many ethnic groups feeling embattled and traumatized, including those within the Russian Federation—in part because they all felt victimized by the Soviet regime. This surely was not a good starting point for state building in multiethnic societies, especially those attempting to introduce sweeping political and economic reforms simultaneously. Over the past several years, different states have had different degrees of success in their nation-building efforts.[4] The record of the Russian Federation is an uneven one. Chechens spent eighteen months fighting to gain recognition of their republic as a sovereign nation, for example, and the final outcome of that bloody civil war is still not fully clear. But dire predictions of the imminent disintegration of the Russian Federation made at the time of the USSR's dissolution have proven unduly pessimistic. This federation is holding together, as the Russian people confront a variety of social and economic crises.

This chapter reviews the recent efforts of the Russian government to mold a national identity for Russia. It discusses the tensions between Russia's continued preoccupation with a nationalities policy and the goal of turning Russia into a more pluralistic and participatory society. It describes how Russia's leaders and ethnic activists have sometimes focused on grievances of the past instead of looking to the future. And it concludes with a look at current efforts to reconcile democracy building with preserving and protecting Russia's ethnic mosaic.

THE CHALLENGE OF RUSSIAN COMPLEXITY

Civic nation building requires that civic loyalty overshadow ethnic particularism, or at least that it coexist with it on equal grounds. Given the importance that ethnicity had in the Soviet era and the role that it still plays in contemporary Russian life, it is unrealistic to expect that a sense of civic loyalty would have fully replaced ethnicity in the seven years since the collapse of the Soviet Union.

Nonetheless, the current state of ethnic relations in Russia is not as discouraging as it is sometimes said to be. The 1993 constitution granted basic civil rights to all citizens and ensured access to the political system for all ethnic groups. Radical non-Russian nationalist groups are not successfully adapting to the new electoral politics, and even Russian nationalist movements, like the Cossacks in southern Russia, are finding it difficult to consolidate as mass political parties. This does not mean that they will fail to do so in the future. The fact that the Russian economic crisis of late 1998 was accompanied by a marked increase in anti-Semitic rhetoric, for example, was an ominous sign. And if social and economic conditions continue to deteriorate, a nationalist-populist figure could still come to power and commit Russia to a policy of national consolidation, restricting rights on ethnic as well as political grounds.

For Russia to be secure as a democratic state there has to be popular consensus on *whom* Russia belongs to and *why*. From the point of view of democratic theory, the ideal answer is that Russia belongs equally to all who live there and hold its citizenship. Those who live outside the state are foreigners. Yet the Russian government is still unwilling to separate fully the question of citizenship from that of ethnicity. It periodically raises the issue of *sootechestvenniki* (ethnic compatriots) in its relations with other post-Soviet states. This pressure diminished over the past few years when it became clear that the leaders of virtually all of the members of the Commonwealth of Independent States (CIS) opposed dual citizenship as undermining the security of their states, especially the presidents of Ukraine, Kazakhstan, and Uzbekistan, whose countries have large numbers of ethnic Russian citizens.

Ethnic Russians living in Russia and in the newly independent states alike are undergoing simultaneous identity crises.[5] The extent to which the two groups decide that they are a single divided people will have an important effect on Russia's foreign and even its domestic politics. Those who seek Russian citizenship often do so as much for economic as for political reasons: many consider holding a Russian passport a prudent strategy in the face of unstable conditions in their country of residence, or, far more frequently, because they have already moved to Russia. Since the passage of the Law on Citizenship of the Russian Federation in 1992, some 1.7 million people have been granted Russian citizenship.[6]

When the post-Soviet states created in December 1991 achieved their independence, the ethno-national communities after which each was named viewed this independence as synonymous with their ethnic empowerment and as their exclusive property. But those who are not from the particular titular ethno-national community also want a role in their new nation's political and cultural definition, as well as the right to participate in its economy on an equal basis.

Most of these people living in the new countries do not see themselves as foreigners, or even as a minority, which is precisely how many from the titular nationality view them, at least in Kazakhstan and Ukraine.[7]

Despite the exclusionary policies adopted by some of these new states and the antagonisms inflamed by political rhetoric from Russia, it appears that the overwhelming majority of Russians living in the Baltic states, Moldova, and Ukraine have managed to combine their ethnic identity with a civic loyalty based mainly on territorial but sometimes also on cultural allegiances. In general, the Soviet legacy of implicit territoriality made the dismemberment of the Soviet Union much less painful than many thought it would be—in large part because of the feelings of civic loyalty that were developing among the people at large. The goal of independence was supported by a substantial part of these old or new nonnative settlers.

The situation within Russia proper is not wholly analogous to that in other post-Soviet states. The Soviet Russian Republic was a federal polity within the USSR, and Russia remains a federal state.[8] Russia's declaration of sovereignty and the 1993 constitution both assert that "the multinational people of Russia" declared an independent state. Many Russian nationalists still argue heatedly that ethnic Russians were the only nation denied self-determination after the breakup of the USSR, when virtually every other group acquired its own state or autonomous territory within Russia.

This is a theme to which the Duma returns repeatedly. In October 1996 the State Duma's Committee on Geopolitics, chaired by Alexei Mitrofanov (a member of Vladimir Zhirinovsky's Liberal Democratic Party of Russia), organized public hearings on whether Russia should be a national state of ethnic Russians. "The main problem demanding urgent solution through federal legislation," Mitrofanov argued at the time, "is a restoration of the legal status of the Russian people *(Russkogo naroda)* and rights according to international principles and norms."[9] In November 1998 the State Duma organized a public hearing on a draft law proclaiming the *Russkaya nasiya* (Russian nation) to be a divided nation, but also a state-forming nation. The initiator of this debate was Oleg Ragozin, a leader of the nationalist Congress of Russian Communities. Ragozin's formulation is implicitly destabilizing for interethnic relations within Russia as well as for its relations with neighboring states, since the non-Russians who make direct linkages between their histories and the states they are forming do not want to accord ethnic Russians any special role in the process.

Several factors make the process of forming a new identity for Russia particularly complex. First, ethnic Russians have a stronger positive identification with the former USSR than do other nationalities. This identification ranges from a formal allegiance to Russia as the legal successor to the USSR to a psychological bond to the USSR as synonymous with historic Russia. Surveys conducted in 1998 by the Institute of Ethnology and Anthropology of the Russian Academy of Sciences showed that 72.3 percent of Russians in Moldova, for example, still identify themselves with their former USSR citizenship. In Russia's Tuva republic, about 50 percent of ethnic Russians (and one-third of the Tuvinians) identify themselves primarily as citizens of the former Soviet Union.

Second, Russia also has a form of institutionalized multiethnicity. Twenty-one of its eighty-nine autonomous formations are simultaneously federal units and nation-states. This is especially true of the units of major non-Russian groups, such as Tatarstan and Bashkortostan.[10] These ethno-political units have been carried over from the Soviet era to the present. During the so-called parade of sovereignties period in 1991–1992, the status of several ethnic autonomous formations was even increased: the Adygei, Altai, and Khakassia autonomous *oblasts*, for example, were constituted as separate republics.[11] In the declarations of sovereignty and in the local and republic constitutions that were adopted in this period, all of the autonomous formations claimed to be sovereign states in the name of all people living in them (for example, in the name of "the Chuvash nation" or the "Udmurt nation").[12] Some declarations and constitutions made no mention of the Russian federal state (Chechnya's declaration of sovereignty, for example), or made a single reference to being associated with the Russian Federation (as in Tatarstan's declaration and constitution).[13]

Russia's top leaders, particularly President Boris Yeltsin, are careful to appeal to the people of Russia (*Rossiyani*) rather than to ethnic Russians (*Russkie*).[14] No one has been entirely successful, however, in explaining what the culture of the *Rossiyani* (pan-Russian) is. And the Russian government continues to monitor alleged acts of discrimination against the 25 million ethnic Russians living in other newly independent states.

CREATING RUSSIAN FEDERALISM

The politicization of ethnicity among small and large ethnic groups led not only to demands for political autonomy and eventually for statehood, but also for control over state resources and assets. Economic motives attracted new participants to the political arena and made ardent nationalists out of many who previously had shown little or no interest in what Michael Ignatieff called "blood and belonging."[15] For the first few years it was not clear how the new Russian state would rein in these new nationalists.

Gradually, the political elites reached some tentative solutions. When members of the Russian Federation signed the Federal Treaty on March 31, 1992, it marked the first time that central and regional authorities agreed on a formula for delimiting power and joint responsibilities in several key areas of governance. The treaty created a new doctrine of federalism for Russia and turned a unitary state into a federal one.[16] It recognized the right of subjects of the federation to exercise a great deal of discretionary authority in the socio-economic and cultural spheres, and to share profits from the economic development of their territories. But these governments were also bound to uphold the provisions of the Russian Constitution.

The document essentially created a legal context for the grassroots declarations of sovereignty by the subjects of the federation, as the Russian government effectively recognized that the subjects of the federation were delegating only a portion of their sovereignty to the central authorities and ignored the fact that such declarations in effect contradicted the then current constitution. The Federal Treaty also established the precedent that Moscow and the republics settle their differences through treaties, like sovereign states. It thus recognized the most important foundation of statehood, and especially federal statehood, which is that power percolates up from below and is transferred on the basis of a social contract. Even more important, the treaty reaffirmed the republics' right to establish the institutional elements of statehood and not just the symbolic ones, as republics were granted the right to create their own constitutions, parliaments, legal codes, and supreme courts.

The Federal Treaty provided for an asymmetric form of federalism. It recognized three different types of constituent federal units: republics; administrative *krais*, *oblasts*, and two federal cities (Moscow and

St. Petersburg); and the autonomous *oblasts* and *okrugs*. While all subjects of the federation were declared to be formally equal in their rights and responsibilities, a greater scope of governance was granted to the republics than to the administrative *krais* and *oblasts*, which in turn were granted greater discretionary authority than the autonomous formations were permitted.

Article II of the Federal Treaty established a long list of shared powers and responsibilities, including provisions on basic human rights, minority rights, preserving the legal order, public security, defense of border zones, division of state property and assets, environmental protection, preserving cultural heritage, education, health care, social welfare, disaster management, and many more issues. Even more important, the treaty granted that there would be joint responsibility for levying and collecting taxes; for administrative, labor, family, land, and housing laws; for the regulation of the use of natural resources; for courts and the police; and for establishing the basic principles of local self-government.

Article III states that "republics (states)"[17] possess all state power (legislative, executive, and judicial) within their territories, albeit only relating to the authority transferred to them by federal organs of power according to the Federal Treaty. Neither the territory nor the status of a republic can be changed without the consent of the republic itself. The article also states that "the land and its resources, water, plant, and animal life belong to the peoples living on the territory of the republic.[18] Thus, the Federal Treaty continued to regard the ethno-territorial autonomous units as composed of ethnic communities rather than of individuals who are simultaneously citizens of these territories and of Russia.

While the constitutions of the various republics avoid claiming that the republics are the homelands of any particular group, they also seek to empower the titular population of the republic by giving prominence to its national language, culture, and history. The result is a de facto second-class status for minority populations (even for those in a majority elsewhere), while also making the titular nationalities feel second-class when they are outside their constituent republics. As awareness of this problem has grown, most prominently in Tatarstan and Sakha (Yakutia), these republics' leaders have made the effort (not always successfully) to create a broader sense of identity based on civic principles, not ethnicity.

During the drafting of the 1993 Russian Constitution, centralists in Moscow made strenuous efforts to overturn or to scale back the provisions of the Federal Treaty. But the treaty remains the cornerstone for regulating center-periphery relations—and is even recognized as such by Article 11 of the Russian Constitution. In the seven years since the Federal Treaty was signed, the subjects of the federation have collectively carved out some fifty areas of exclusive authority.[19]

For some leaders in the republics, the Federal Treaty did not go far enough. The leadership of Tatarstan negotiated its own separate treaty, which was signed in February 1994. The Dudaev government in Chechnya refused to recognize the authority of the Russian Federation on its territory—and dared Russia to do something about it. And from the beginning, Russia has found it difficult to get even the more moderate subjects of the federation to reconcile their laws and practices with provisions of the Russian Constitution or with legislative acts and presidential and government decrees. Yet, with the conspicuous exception of Chechnya, the Russian government has tried to wear down regional and republic resistance to central authority rather than confronting it outright.

By December 1994 the government in Moscow felt secure enough about the stability of the remaining center-periphery relationships to go to war with Chechnya, the one holdout republic. The decision to finish off the last remaining direct threat to Russia's federal structure and territorial integrity had as much to do with restoring popular support for President Yeltsin through a successful military campaign as it did with maintaining the constitutional integrity of the country. The war was certainly a human catastrophe and a military failure; it nonetheless helped demonstrate the stability of the Russian Federation. Not one of Russia's regional governments supported the cause of Chechnya's secession—or demanded that future concessions to Chechnya be applied to it as well.

At the same time, public reaction to the Chechnya War showed how little enthusiasm there was for fighting to keep Russia intact. There were many causes of the war's unpopularity, not the least of which was lingering confusion over whether Chechnya was a part of Russia, and if so, what price should be paid to keep it. Several republican leaders publicly expressed their disagreement with the massive use of military force against a breakaway region, particularly presidents Mintimer Shamiev of Tatarstan, Ruslan Aushev of

Ingushetia, and Nikolai Fedorov of Chuvashia. The Chechnya War brought additional confusion to the process of identity formation, as it crystallized two mutually exclusive tendencies. The war made it clear that the Russian Federation is not immune to the pressures of separatism, and thus must provide a special status for potentially powerful autonomous non-Russian territories. At the same time, the war helped popularize statist or Russian nationalist ideologues who argue for maintaining the territorial integrity of Russia and for neutralizing potential risks to that integrity before they gain the power to do real damage.

The Chechnya War exacerbated the economic and political challenges faced by the Russian government. It deepened the sense of division between the indigenous communities of the North Caucasus and the rest of the country, as the phrase "Russia and North Caucasus" became common parlance, making the latter seem as if it were not a part of the former. It has also made it more rather than less difficult for Russians to determine whether Russia is the single, shared homeland of all who live there—or a collection of distinct ethnic homelands.

IMPROVISING A NEW DOCTRINE

The relationship between citizenship and nationality has changed in important ways since Russian independence. In the Soviet Union, citizenship was distinct from nationality. Everyone was a Soviet citizen, but no one was a Soviet national. Ethnic identity defined people's most cherished values and traits and served as the most effective base for social coalitions, including the constitution of a state.

For this reason, most former Soviet citizens intuitively believe that the breakup of the Soviet Union had led to a fusion of nationality and citizenship. This belief created problems for ethnic minorities who comprise about one-fifth of the total population of the former Soviet Union. The implicit identification of ethnic origin with citizenship makes many of these people feel that they are second-class citizens. This is especially true for those whose native tongue was Russian rather than the local national language. Nation-states created out of multiethnic Soviet republics have de facto institutionalized a set of relationships in which the political loyalty of ethnic minorities will always be more suspect than that of the majority. While this is a problem everywhere in the former Soviet Union, it is especially salient in Russia. By virtue of its status as a federation, Russia must resolve a more complicated relationship between nation and statehood than must the other successor states. It is a relationship that is only partly worked out and that the first Russian government was ill-prepared to confront.

The government of acting prime minister Yegor Gaidar may have had well defined proposals for economic and political reform, but on nationalities issues it basically improvised.[20] While some observers might have seen the efforts of ethnic groups to achieve national self-determination as a victory for liberal ideals, most within Russia's political establishment viewed such efforts as destructive of Russian statehood. Part of the establishment also wanted to expand the definition of Russian statehood to include all those whose ethnic roots lay within Russia—even if they now live in the other countries. As a result, many who lived in Russia (mostly ethnic Russians but also Avars, Armenians, Ossets, and others) sympathized with and in some cases sought aid for secessionist forces in Transdniester, Karabakh, South Ossetia, and Abkhazia.[21]

The confusion over how to define Russian statehood was inevitable. In any new political nation, parochial loyalties are likely to overpower universalist ones. Russia is not simply a new nation, but also the continuation of an older one, in which the creation of a new universalist identity must bear the weight of past legacies. There was some sense of shared or universalist identity in the Russian Empire and in the Soviet state, although in both cases people preserved multiple identities as well. These identities, though, were largely discredited, and a new justification for a universalist identity had to be found.

President Yeltsin's primary goal in the tough political climate of 1991–1993 was to shore up support in the periphery for the idea of a renewed Russian Federation. Guided more by the imperatives of holding power than by the principles of civic nation building, Yeltsin struck bargains and made substantial concessions to advance his goal of a democratic Russia. But many of the concrete steps that were taken in the area of nationalities policy seemed contradictory.

Most of the contradictions in Russia's type of federalism are the results of decisions made in 1991–1992 by a bicameral Supreme

Soviet in which one house (the Council of Nationalities) was domi-nated by a large number of former Communist *nomenklatura* leaders of various nationalities, as well as by activists of the radical ethno-nationalist movements of the periphery. Both of these groups were inexperienced in lawmaking and ill-prepared for the challenge of managing ethnic issues.

In April 1991, for example, the Supreme Soviet of the Russian SFSR passed the Law on the Rehabilitation of Repressed Peoples. It gave peoples who had been forcibly deported from traditional territories the right to return to those lands, and it promised them compensation for their suffering. Some of this compensation was to take the form of special benefits, such as increased pensions and tripled credit for time spent working in places of exile.[22]

In June 1992 the president of the Supreme Soviet proposed divid-ing the Checheno-Ingush Republic into two separate ethnic forma-tions, but no guidelines were offered for drawing boundaries of the new Ingush republic. This contributed to a general worsening of ethnic relations in the North Caucasus and led to the November 1992 clash in the disputed Prigorodny *rayon* (district) of North Ossetia on the border of the Ingush republic that left 800 people dead and created 40,000 refugees.[23]

These policies also encouraged the migration of ethnic communi-ties back to their so-called homelands, which created new grievances among others who had long ago settled in their places and who now thought of these regions as their homes. A potentially explosive situation developed in the Volga region in November 1991, when President Boris Yeltsin, during his first official visit to Germany, signed with Chancellor Helmut Kohl an official document calling for the re-creation of the Volga German Republic. This republic had been dissolved in 1941, when it was absorbed into the Volgograd and Saratov *oblasts*. Fifty years later it was home to fewer than 2 percent of Russia's Germans. The idea of reviving the republic (which was later dropped) was a response to demands from Volga German leaders for their own state—but also an attempt to gain foreign assistance from the Federal Republic of Germany, whose government was eager to create economic opportunities for the for-mer USSR's German population (most of whom had settled in Russia back in the eighteenth century) so that they would not request repa-triation to Germany.

These policy initiatives served as a tacit endorsement of the idea that the post-Soviet world would be divided in much the same way the Soviet world had been. The goal was to purge Russian society of communism rather than to build new forms of political loyalty. Radical nationalists would be tolerated as long as they were anticommunist. Thus, in the fall of 1991—with the participation of such democratic activists as Gennady Burbulis, Ruslan Khasbulatov, Mikhail Poltoranin, and Galina Starovoitova—the former communist official Doku Zavgaev was replaced by the so-called democrat General Dzhokar Dudaev in Checheno-Ingushetia. This change of leadership, coupled with the loss of central control over the army arsenal, ended the fragile stability in Chechnya and showed just how little the Russian elite understood about the socio-cultural and political dynamics in periphery regions.

Russian parliamentarians also were confused about how to handle issues of minority rights and interethnic conflict. In 1992–1993, the Committee on Interethnic Relations of the Supreme Soviet of the Russian Federation drafted a law on minorities that would have given additional state support and legal protection not to indigenous people in national territories, such as the Komi, Chukchi, and Karel peoples (who presumably were protected by their new national-statehood status) but to other ethnic groups living there, including Russians and Ukrainians. This law was not passed by the Duma, mainly because of the legislators' inability to agree on a definition of a minority in a federation of nations. It was not until June 1998 that the Duma ratified the convention on the rights of national minorities of the Organization on Security and Cooperation in Europe, and even then it did so without defining the status of minority groups in Russia.

Legislative assistance for indigenous Northern groups known as the "small peoples" of Siberia (because they are few in numbers) was also put at risk by some of their traditional advocates, who tried to get Russia to abide by supposed international norms in dealing with the deteriorating circumstances of these Arctic peoples. Some members of the Supreme Soviet's Committee on the Small Peoples, which included some leaders of the Northern peoples, wanted Russia to abide by provisions of the International Labor Organization's 1989 Declaration on the Rights of the Indigenous Peoples. This set of policy guidelines was drawn up by those most familiar with the conditions of Native Americans and Circumpolar peoples and assumed a developed industrial economy capable of sustaining small fragile cultures. The debate over this declaration once again highlighted the confusion over how to understand the common good in a nation that still perceives itself as a collection of ethno-nations, and in which Russians are the largest but not always the most strategically located group.

The list of potential quandaries over the control of resources and state assets raised by the prevailing legislative views was almost endless. Should Arctic oil be extracted even if so doing would disrupt local economies based on reindeer and other wildlife migration patterns? Who owns the Sakha Republic's diamonds or gold? To whom do the trees of Mari El belong, and should they be conserved or felled? Given how great the potential economic rewards were, the proponents of collective rights had a real incentive to offer supporters: winning gave them the right to administer and even to privatize the collective wealth. The new Russian legal system inherited the notion of the collective right of ethnoses and so institutionalized new sources of conflict, since it was not the way of life of a citizen but rather his or her blood provenance or registered nationality that became the source of an individual's economic as well as political status. There is another irony behind the dilemma. Quite often it is not natives but local economic barons and politicians of Russian or of other European origin who exploit the rights supposedly assigned to indigenous communities for their own good—as in the Chukotka and Komi republics or in Khanty-Mansy autonomous *okrug*. In other regions, for example the North Caucasus, representatives of non-Russian nationalities (well-educated and with Soviet-era experiences of underground private entrepreneurship) have been able to dominate the process of economic transition. Thus, the introduction of economic reforms and the general atmosphere of political liberation have created new roles for ethnic communities and have encouraged new forms of competition to develop around the ethnic factor.

AN UNTIMELY REFORM PROPOSAL

While issues of ethnicity and nationality were not the central concerns of Prime Minister Gaidar's team (which was then concentrating on major economic and political reforms), there was a growing sense in the government that the radical (and implicitly ethno-nationalist) version of democratic ideology that many had advocated at the time of the USSR's collapse was inconsistent with a number of key political goals. In 1992 President Yeltsin requested that the State Committee on Nationalities Policy draft a concept paper on these issues. Work began at the federal Ministry of Nationalities in the spring of 1992, and the draft paper was presented by one of the authors of this chapter at a cabinet meeting on July 30, 1992.

The document was deliberately made as nonconfrontational as possible and was designed to leave room for flexibility in a radically changing society. The terms "peoples," "nationalities," and "ethno-cultural entities" were used as substitutes for the more emotionally charged terms "nation" and "minority," and the terminology was no longer used in a hierarchical way.[24] Since only 47 percent of non-Russians lived in the territories of their republics, the proposal called for Russia's nationalities policy to apply to the entire territory of the Russian Federation and to all of its population, including ethnic Russians.

Ethnic Russians themselves faced the challenge of cultural regeneration in the aftermath of Soviet communist rule. In some places they were becoming cultural minorities or experiencing social degradation, especially in the newly independent states, but also in parts of Russia itself. In the draft document, both types of Russian minority communities were referred to in noninflammatory language to counter the continuing exploitation of this issue by Russian nationalists.

A policy of cultural pluralism, a sort of "unity in diversity," was proposed as a unifying formula for multiethnic Russia. The power and resources of the state, at both the federal and local levels, were said to belong to all people, not to any particular ethnic group. The center, which included all the political, cultural, and media institutions, was expected to reflect the ethnic mosaic of the entire state. And control over political and economic resources in the republics should not be usurped by the representatives of one nationality, but should reflect the multiethnic composition of the entire population. The document also recommended that the representation of non-Russian peoples and cultures be expanded at the center of the nation's political and cultural life. Moscow should introduce radio broadcasting in the languages of the other large peoples of Russia

(Tatars, Buryats, Chuvash, Chechens, and others), for example, and should increase these peoples' visibility on television.

The document also recommended broadening the rights of Russia's other territorial administrative units (*krais* and *oblasts*) to make all of the subjects of the federation roughly equal to the republics. Since it was clear that Russia was decentralizing authority, regional governments also had to show greater sensitivity toward the cultural demands and needs of all of Russia's citizens.

The draft also made reference to rights of extra-territorial cultural autonomy, which applied outside the existing ethno-territorial boundaries. This idea had been strongly condemned in Bolshevik nationalities theory, and even in 1992 it was still viewed as heretical. The draft defended this form of autonomy as a way for the state to support the development of cultures and to protect the rights of all ethnic groups. The existing territorially based form of autonomy did not provide adequate protection for any of the country's ethnic communities, because administrative and republic boundaries did not correspond to the geographic distribution of minority populations. The substitution of a broader understanding of cultural rights for the existing exclusively territorial one would have brought Russian practice closer to that of other developed democracies. This, however, was not a priority at the time. In the end, the Russian government simply failed to act on this document.

SIGNS OF CONSENSUS

Four years later, a substantially revised white paper on ethnicity and nationalism was prepared; this time, the draft was supported by republic leaders and approved by the government (on April 11, 1996) and signed by President Yeltsin (on June 15).[25]

The new document identifies Russia as a "civic nation." It permits leaders of the republics or the activists of ethno-cultural communities to use the term *nation* in its ethno-cultural sense, but reserves to Russia itself the right to use the term *nation* in its international political-legal meaning. The term *narod* (the people) is used in its ethnic sense, not in the sense of a civic community of the entire population, as is the more common meaning in developed democracies. A *narod* is a group of individuals who recognize themselves as sharing a common culture, language, historic memory, or the belief that they have a common origin. There is no implicit tension between the civic and the ethno-cultural meaning of *narod*, and individuals can identify with both types of communities simultaneously and support other communal memberships as well.

Problems may begin, however, when ethnic identity (or ethno-cultural community membership) takes on an explicitly political meaning, as when an ethno-cultural community claims the right of national self-determination. The most radical form of self-determination, of course, is political independence. But claims of self-determination short of independence can be accommodated within the structures of a multiethnic state through such measures as granting extra-territorial autonomy.[26]

The Russian Federation has attempted to solve the problem of national self-determination through a form of ethnic federalism that recognizes that there will be multiple and disparate relations between the center and the subjects of the federation.[27] The Russian Constitution does not grant its constituent republics the right to secession, and it proclaims the superiority of federal law over all other laws. But many of the republic constitutions (those of Tuva and Tatarstan, for example) also claim that their republic laws are supreme and implicitly assert an unlimited right of self-determination. Reconciling potentially conflicting constitutions and bodies of laws is one of Russia's foremost political challenges: about 70 percent of the regional legislative acts passed since 1991 in the republics, *oblasts,* and *krais* contradict federal legislation. To some degree this challenge is mediated by bilateral treaties and agreements (approximately thirty of which were in effect by the end of 1997), but the problem remains a serious one.[28]

The white paper explored other options for expressing self-determination, including offering ethno-cultural communities legal protections that are independent of their territory. These might include special forms of political representation, legislative initiative, multiple educational systems, distinct patterns of property ownership, and even indigenous legal codes.

In December 1996 the State Duma enacted at least some of the ideas in the white paper when it passed the Law on National-Cultural Autonomy. But the new law still linked the concepts of cultural and territorial autonomy by restricting each ethnic group to only one cultural autonomous association at the federal level and by insisting that these associations be linked to the local, regional, or federal levels. The law has stimulated the establishment of a large number of extraterritorial ethnic coalitions, especially in large cities and in *oblasts* and *krais* with multiethnic populations. In Moscow alone, there are several dozen national-cultural autonomous associations of Ukrainians, Volga Germans, Koreans, Tatars, and others. But the challenge of building a truly multiethnic civic nation in Russia remains to be met by some future government.

LEGISLATING ETHNIC HARMONY

States do not exist solely because of their written constitutions, secured borders, printed passports, and international recognition. Their existence also depends upon the loyalty of their citizens to the territorial and cultural projection of the state. Different societies tolerate different degrees of cultural diversity, in part in response to their varying self-images. In some societies that are considered homogeneous, these differences are not noticeable, while in others they make themselves painfully clear. Not every society attaches primordial meaning to ethnos and ethnic diversity or views these characteristics as fundamental to its members' identity.

The goal of managing interethnic relations in the Soviet successor states cannot be separated from the goal of creating civic identities. Democratic societies strive to find ways to support both the ethnic and the civic identities of their citizens. The surest path to stable ethnic relations within Russia, Ukraine, Moldova, or Kazakhstan would be through the creation of all-Russian, all-Ukrainian, all-Moldovan, or all-Kazakh identities. This would also be the most democratic solution, as it would balance individual and collective rights.

Many experts think that federalism offers the best chance of stability for multiethnic societies. Russia is the only one of the fifteen newly independent states to declare itself a federation. De facto forms of territorial autonomy exist in Azerbaijan, Georgia, Ukraine, Uzbekistan, and Moldova, but, of these states, only Georgia has been willing to discuss formal federative arrangements. Eventually, each of these states may have to consider some type of federative arrangement. For the foreseeable future it is unlikely to come under serious discussion, since in most of the newly independent states, democratic reform is generally seen as a less pressing goal than ethnic consolidation.

Russian federalism is in reality a form of ethno-territorial autonomy in which republics function as quasi-nation states and reflect
the claims of a certain ethnic group to the territory it populates.
Ethnic federalism presupposes that the population of a particular
autonomy is composed of a homogeneous ethnic group, or at least
that an ethnic group has a clear majority among this population.
But in many of Russia's ethno-territorial units, this is not currently
the case. When it is the case, ethnic federalism is not in profound
conflict with democratic principles and need not undermine civic
loyalty, since policies of ethnic cohesion and preferences are also
reflective of majority rule.

There are several important differences between the situation in
Russia and in other ethnic federations, such as India, Canada, or
Spain.[29] The most important difference is that citizens of Russia do
not yet have some form of dual identity like the Basques and Catalans
in Spain or the Quebecois in Canada. Russians also lack a notion
comparable to that of "an Indian nation"—although in some ways
they came closer to this in Soviet times than they do today.[30] The
term *Rossiyan* (pan-Russian) conveys a sense of this dual identity,
which is becoming more commonplace and instinctive, especially as
those in the republics become more satisfied with their new political
status and center.

Not all of Russia's titular nationalities have been passive observers
while federal policy makers search for new formulas for governing
their multiethnic societies. Creative constitutionally based solutions
for sharing power among ethnic groups have emerged in several
parts of Russia, including Sakha (Yakutia), Buryatia, Tatarstan,
Kabardino-Balkaria, and several *oblasts* and regions. One such creative innovation was Daghestan's collective elected presidency,
which rotates on an ethnic basis. This arrangement was undermined,
though, when the Constitutional Court of Russia supported
Magomedali Magomedov's refusal to give up power at the end of
his rotation. The histories of states like Lebanon, not to mention
Yugoslavia, illustrate the potentially short-lived success of formulas
based on rotation or on achieving an ethnic balance in top leadership
positions. Nonetheless, there is some merit in trying to prevent, even
in the short run, the further politicization of ethnic divisions at a
time of rapid economic and political change. Major ethnic communities that feel left out of the political process have a strong incentive
to destabilize the status quo.

Another unresolved dilemma of ethnic federalism is how to preserve the distinct ethno-cultural profiles of the autonomous regions of Russia, where the titular ethnic groups are not a decisive majority, without imposing territorial changes or discriminating against other ethnic groups. The symbolic importance of statehood for these groups is so great that their cultural integrity could be put at risk if the distinct national or cultural profiles of these republics is not preserved.

One way to preserve this cultural integrity would be to develop institutions that encourage people to function in two or more local cultural systems—by learning another language, for example. Some of the republics are already laying the foundations for this: the president of Tatarstan must speak Tatar but need not be an ethnic Tatar. An analogous provision is found in the constitution of several other republics, where the right to hold office is not restricted on the basis of consanguinity but is open to all who are willing to function in the local cultural system.

Another way that multiethnic societies protect group interests is through formal power sharing arrangements by ethnic group representatives, as in the so-called consociational democracies of Austria, Belgium, Switzerland, and the Netherlands (all of which are small and physically compact countries). To introduce such arrangements in Russia, however, would put pressure on tens of millions of people to decide their group membership. It might also make group boundaries more rigid, stimulate the development of ethnic parties, promote formal discrimination, and reduce the likelihood that people would become multilingual and multicultural.

In a country as large and ethnically diverse as Russia, human bridges between ethnic communities are essential. Russia's citizens should be free to preserve their unique cultures or to assimilate into the dominant Russian culture and language. Democratization means that cross-ethnic governing coalitions must be created on a multicultural basis. Such steps do not in any way undermine the existence and significance of ethno-cultural entities.[31]

Cultural dialogue and interaction were always features of Soviet and hence of Russian life. The patterns of such dialogue and interaction in the Russian Federation must change to reflect new political and economic goals. Russia already has adopted an integrationist approach. The current government seeks to distribute power among the various groups more through informal means than through formal quotas, as would be the case in a consociational democracy. But even though consociational democracy does not appear to be practical for Russia, some elements of it may be approximated by elite agreements on informal power-sharing or by balancing ethnic representation in certain governing bodies.

Nonetheless, the introduction of fixed or informal ethnic quotas will not resolve the issue of representation for non-Russians in leadership positions. As the behavior of Russia's current political elite demonstrates, it is a mistake to assume either the homogeneity of ethnic groups or the loyalty of elites to their ethnic communities. The viability of Russia's current ad hoc and formal arrangements will depend in large part on the quality of the leadership exercised by representatives from the peripheries themselves.

FROM ETHNIC TO CIVIC NATIONALISM

The way that ethno-national terms were used in the Soviet context helped foster a sense of *we* and *they*. It pressed people to define what was familiar and alien using ethnic criteria. Some terms that are still in common usage in Russia and other post-Soviet states—such as ethnos, superethnos, subethnic groups, or national groups—serve to stimulate conflicts. They put basic civil rights at risk and ironically make it more difficult to adopt basic laws safeguarding interests and human rights of citizens who belong to particular cultural communities. In 1997, for example, the Russian government delayed issuing new passports because of a controversy over references to nationality in the documents; the European Convention on Citizenship, to which Russia had acceded, precludes the linkage of citizenship with ethnic origin. Even the question of what symbol to put on the passport was highly controversial: many Russians objected to replacing the Soviet Union's hammer-and-sickle insignia with the Imperial Russian double eagle.[32]

The difficulties in defining "the nation" come from trying to convert an emotional state into an objective category. In today's Russia, nationalism or ethno-nationalism is still based on the conviction that a nation is a form of ethnic entity whose membership is constructed on deep historical characteristics, and that this ethnic collective empowers the formation of a state with all of its institutions, resources, and a cultural system. At the same time, once created, the state develops its own imperatives, including the perceived right to define the nation. Thus, in the end, the state and these ethno-cultural constructs find themselves in a competition that realistically can never be fully resolved.

This tension can either lead to transformed identities or to civil conflict. Whatever claims ethno-nationalists may make to the contrary, the linkage between these ethno-cultural constructs is no less fragile than the idea of the nation itself. The truth is that in any such ethno-cultural group (Russians, Tatars, Buryats, or Yakuts, for example), elite elements are able to mobilize the mass national consciousness through the use of words and other symbols of self-identification. The current political climate can create powerful incentives for invoking these ethno-cultural categories. More than a dozen ethnic communities in Dagestan alone use the word *nation* to describe their ethnic entities, as do political leaders and cultural elites of ethnic communities like the Karaim and Nanait, which consist of only several hundred members.

Both senses of the term *nation* — the cultural or ethno-nation, and the civic or political nation—can coexist during times of transformation. But there is always the danger that legal codifications will make ethno-political groupings more rigid. Encouraging the development of the civic nation metaphor would seem to be a prudent way to promote political stability in most multiethnic societies. To date, Russian public debates have not focused on the problem of civic nationalism; most people still think about nationalism in ethnic rather than in civic or state terms. There is some reference to a civic nation in the rhetoric of state patriotism, at least with regard to the dominant Russian nation, as when Russian ethno-nationalists try to usurp the metaphor of *Rossiya* (pan-Russian nation) as the exclusive property of *Russkie* (ethnic Russians). In this specific case, there is a vague and poorly articulated distinction made between ethnic and civic nationalism. But the formulation is provocative because it effectively excludes all non-Russians from the core of the Russian state.

Nevertheless, there is some reason to believe that the Russian public, possibly even sooner than the political elites, will recognize that the common needs of Russian state building should predominate over those of ethnic particularism. There are plenty of reasons to accept the existence of an all-Russian civic entity and to make efforts to strengthen it. The consciousness of ordinary people is more inclusive than the consciousness and norms of intellectual and political elites.[33]

Over time, one can expect a new understanding of how the nation-state is to evolve in Russia, one that defines national characteristics in ways that strengthen state legitimacy. It is easy to exaggerate the uniqueness of one's own state and culture, as well as the homogeneity of other societies. The process of creating civic patriotism in multiethnic Russia need not be fundamentally different from the process in other nations such as Mexico, Spain, Malaysia, Indonesia, or India. Russia's choice to retain a federal form of government will certainly influence the process and will likely even slow it, but the challenge of civil incorporation is essentially the same worldwide.

The process of state building in Russia will certainly be influenced by holdover intellectual categories and institutional structures from the Soviet period. All societies are shaped by past actions as well as by present ones. It is time, however, for Russians to free themselves from an undue preoccupation with their past and from finding fault or attributing blame on the basis of it. The quicker those who live in and study Russia come to realize this, the easier the problem of civic-nation building will become.

Russia is a multiethnic state. But every consolidating nation-state in Western Europe, Latin America, Asia, and Africa was also—and still is—a multiethnic state. The fact that Russia is composed of a rich mosaic of ethnic communities should not cast doubt on the legitimacy of the state or justify ethno-nationalism in the periphery. It is unfortunate that in the effort to ward off further acts of secession, Russian politicians chose to make reference in the constitution to the "nations" of Russia rather than to Russia's many cultures or peoples. By talking of Russia's nations they have found a linguistic formulation that emphasizes political rivalry rather than political cooperation.

A state that is a coalition with more rigid territorial borders and fixed citizenship has more reasons to call itself a nation than does a coalition based on ethnic identity. A state has a public mandate to use legitimate force and has the relevant institutions, resources, and laws to advance the cause of its survival, while ethnic communities have vague boundaries and their members are subject to multiple and even conflicting identities.

Over time, inevitably, the most powerful social coalition will be able to monopolize the use of this term, as well as to determine the meaning of the *Rossiyan* (pan-Russian) nation-state. It is far from certain that the ethnic dimension will be the sole determinant of what the Russian nation-state will become. The process of civic-nation building is certain to be far more complex, and is likely to produce an outcome that is acceptable to members of the multiethnic community of Russia, particularly if they view it as a form of protection rather than as a violation of their rights.

Ethno-nationalism cannot, and perhaps should not, be destroyed by state decrees. In its cultural and political forms, ethno-nationalism has played a positive role—for example, in aiding the decentralization of power, preserving cultural identity, and maintaining the integrity of ethnic groups. Today, ethno-nationalism compensates for the lack of democracy and civic loyalty. It can be weakened and abolished only through the improvement of social conditions of existence and governance based on cultural pluralism and the principle of "unity in diversity."

The most serious obstacle to establishing civic nationalism or all-Russian patriotism is not so much the nationalism of the non-Russians as it is nationalism in the name of the "Russian nation" as the state forming, uniting, *superethnos*. The notion of the Russian nation in its ethnic form is both relatively new and of elite design: it is a response to the opportunity to declare openly that Russia is a political nation. The vast majority of the Russian citizens who consider themselves Russian are content to be part of a Russian people or culture and are not pressing for the use of more politicized categories. The question of nation-state building in Russia, therefore, is not synonymous with the liquidation or abolition of nationalities and ethnoses. It is a process that is independent of the question of the preservation and development of Russian culture, and can be made independent of the preservation and development of Russia's other cultures as well.

The challenge Russia faces is to establish a set of overlapping ethnic and civic identities, so that loyalty to a particular culture does not conflict with loyalty to Russia as a political entity. According to the results of numerous ethno-political studies, identification with and loyalty to Russia is actually quite strong, despite the partially preserved Soviet identity and growing cultural and regional particularism.[34] But an effective policy agenda based on this identification and loyalty has yet to be developed. It is clearly time for Russia's academics and policy makers to discard the old Soviet vocabulary of ethno-nationalism and to begin using more neutral and internationally acceptable terminology that shows greater sensitivity toward the phenomenon of ethnicity.

Other Soviet successor states may choose to empower the ethnonationalism of the dominant nationality as the foundation of their civic patriotism. The success of these efforts is by no means assured in every case. This cannot be an acceptable strategy of state building in Russia. Russia is a federation, and backing away from this in Russia's current political environment is a likely recipe for civil war. While the nation's political elites seem to recognize this clearly, they too are products of the old Soviet system they vowed to change. While they may invoke the rhetoric of civic loyalty on public occasions, most still think of themselves in ethnic terms. With the fires of the Chechnya War still not fully extinguished, ethno-nationalism seems very much a part of contemporary Russian life.

Interethnic relations in Russia remain hierarchical, although less hierarchical than during the Soviet days. For all its invocation of its thousand-year history, modern Russia is still a young state. As the Russian polity matures, these perceived ethnic hierarchies will hopefully become modified, as they have in other developed multiethnic industrial democracies. Ethnicity and ethnic consciousness never disappear, but ethno-nationalism abates when individuals feel politically empowered without reference to their ethnic origin. The Russian state has set both this and the simultaneous protection of ethnic communities as its goals. These goals are admirable, and if the current and succeeding regimes make them priorities, civic loyalty may become as much a fact of Russian political life within a generation or two as ethnic consciousness is today.

Russia has made real strides toward attaining these goals in its first years of statehood, but these strides have been made at enormous cost. According to the most conservative estimates, the war in Chechnya left more than 35,000 dead and more than 500,000 refugees. The economy of Chechnya was left in ruins; numerous schools, museums, and libraries were destroyed. The Chechens will need generations to recover from the devastation; Russians too will need a long time to recover from the trauma of their defeat and the brutality of their actions.[35]

At the same time, the scale of this tragedy has served to stabilize intercommunal relations. Russia's major ethno-national communities enjoy greater communal protection than ever before because the constitution and provisions of the Federal Treaty grant their territorial governments substantial rights to collect and spend revenue. There is no longer serious talk of secession from Russia; for now at least, those who want to strip the republics of their power accept the dangers of confrontation as too great. The end result is certainly a compromise from the viewpoint of democratic theory: many of the republics are governed less democratically than Russia as a whole. In today's Russia, guarantees of cultural self-determination are more important than those of political pluralism, although it is hard to predict what tensions may develop in the future over this trade-off. Eight years is certainly too short a time for Russia to have solved its nationalities problem. It may, however, be long enough to have taught its leaders how to keep the country from further violent implosions.

NOTES

[1] See Martha Brill Olcott, "Yuri Andropov and the 'National Problem'," *Soviet Studies*, vol. 37 (January 1985), pp. 103–17; Gail W. Lapidus, "Gorbachev's Nationalities Problem," *Foreign Affairs* (Fall 1989), pp. 92–108; Yuri Slezkine, "The USSR as a Communal Apartment, or How a Socialist State Promoted Ethnic Particularism," *Slavic Review*, vol. 53, no. 2, Summer 1994, pp. 414–52.

[2] See Yulian Bromley and Viktor Kozlov, "The Theory of Ethnos and Ethnic Processes in Soviet Social Sciences," *Comparative Studies in Society and History*, vol. 31, no. 3, July 1989, pp. 425–38. For a critique, see Peter Skalnik, "Soviet Ethnography and the national(ities) question," *Cahiers du Monde russe et sovietique*, vol. XXXI (2–3), April–September 1990, pp. 183–92.

[3] John Dunlop, *The Faces of Contemporary Russian Nationalism* (Princeton: Princeton University Press, 1983).

[4] For a general overview of nationalities, see Ian Bremmer and Ray Taras, eds., *New States, New Politics: Building the Post-Soviet Nations* (Cambridge, UK: Cambridge University Press, 1997). On Russia, see Valery Tishkov, *Ethnicity, Nationalism, and Conflicts In and After the Soviet Union: The Mind Aflame* (London: Sage Publications,

1997). On Central Asia, see Martha Brill Olcott, *Central Asia's New States: Independence, Foreign Policy, and Regional Security* (Washington, D.C.: United States Institute of Peace Press, 1996). On the Baltics, see Anatol Lieven, *The Baltic Revolution: Estonia, Latvia, Lithuania, and the Path to Independence* (New Haven: Yale University Press, 1993).

5 The most recent studies are David D. Laitin, *Identity in Formation: The Russian-Speaking Populations in the Near Abroad* (Ithaca: Cornell University Press, 1998); Charles King and Neil J. Melvin, eds., *Nations Abroad: Diaspora Politics and International Relations in the Former Soviet Union* (Boulder, Colo.: Westview Press, 1998); Lubov Ostapenko and Irma Subbotina, *Russkie v Moldavii: Adaptatsiya ili Migratsiya* (Moscow: Institute of Ethnology and Anthropology, 1998); and Galina Vitkovskaya, ed., *Sovremenniye etnopoliticheskie protsessy i migratsionnaya situatsiya v Tsentral'noi Azii* (Moscow: Carnegie Moscow Center, 1998).

6 Some 123,000 people were granted Russian citizenship in 1992–1993, 444,000 in 1994, 702,000 in 1995, and 490,000 in 1996. It is estimated that 80 percent of these are ethnic Russians.

7 Mikhail N. Guboglo, "Etnopoliticheskaya situatsiya v Kazakhstane," in E. M. Kozhokin, ed., *Kazakhstan: realii i perspektivy nezavisimogo razvitiya* (Moscow: Russian Institute of Strategic Studies, 1995).

8 Russia's official name in the USSR was the Russian Soviet Federative Socialist Republic (RSFSR).

9 Author's notes of a speech by Alexei Mitrofanov before the State Duma Committee on Geopolitics, Moscow, November 1, 1996. On the doctrine and practice of dominant Russian ethno-nationalism, see Valery Tishkov, "Post-Soviet Nationalism," in Richard Caplan and John Feffer, eds., *Europe's New Nationalism: States and Minorities in Conflict* (New York: Oxford University Press, 1996). See also John Dunlop, *The Faces of Contemporary Russian Nationalism* (Princeton: Princeton University Press, 1983).

10 These twenty-one republics contain one-third of the total territory of the Russian republic and account for 16 percent of the nation's total population. Overall, 40 percent of the population of these republics is drawn from the titular nationality, and 43.7 percent are Russians. In nine of the twenty-one republics the titular nationality enjoys majority status.

[11] The Russian Federation is made up of twenty-one republics (*respubliki*), six territories (*kraia*), forty-nine regions (*oblasti*), one Jewish autonomous region (*avtonomnaya oblast*), ten autonomous areas (*avtonomniye okruga*), and two "cities of federal importance," Moscow and St. Petersburg.

[12] In the case of those north Caucasian republics that bear the names of two nationalities, this claim was said to be consistent with an act of national self-determination of both peoples.

[13] Such actions are also consistent with the experience of African and Asian countries such as South Africa and India. See Timothy Sisk, *Power Sharing and International Mediation in Ethnic Conflicts* (Washington, D.C.: United States Institute of Peace Press, 1996); Arend Liphart, *Democracy in Plural Societies* (New Haven: Yale University Press, 1977); Crawford Young, *The Rising Tide of Cultural Pluralism: The Nation-State at Bay?* (Madison: University of Wisconsin Press, 1993). On the historic experience of ethnocultural autonomy in Russia, see M. N. Guboglo and I. V. Nam, eds., *Natsional'no - kul'turnye avtonomii i ob'edineniya: istoriographiya, politika, praktika*, vol. I–III (Moscow: Institute of Ethnography and Anthropology, 1995).

[14] In the Russian language, *Russkie* is the word for ethnic Russians while *Rossiyani* (pan-Russian) is an ethnically neutral term describing all those who live in *Rossiya* (Russia). The relationship between these terms is not well-established; *Rossiyani* is common in formal statements, while *Russkie* is used more frequently in informal settings.

[15] Michael Ignatieff, *Blood and Belonging: Journeys into the New Nationalism* (London: Chatto and Windus, 1993).

[16] The formal title is the Treaty on Demarcating Objects of Jurisdiction and Powers between the Federal Bodies of State Power of the Russian Federation and the Bodies of Power of the Republics within the Russian Federation.

[17] The Russian text reads "respubliki (gosudarstva)," implying the state power of the republic.

[18] *Federativnyi dogovor. Dokumenty. Kommentarii* (Moscow: Respublika, 1992), p. 13.

[19] Vladimir Lysenko, "Kakuiu federatsiiu my postroili," *Nezavisimaya gazeta*, March 28, 1997, p. 2.

20 Gaidar was deputy prime minister for economics and finance from 1991 to 1994. He served as acting prime minister from June to December 1992.

21 Transdniester is a region of Moldova in which the ethnic Russian majority has declared its independence and has received military support from Russia in its efforts. Karabakh (also called Nagorno-Karabakh) is an ethnic Armenian region of Azerbaijan. After separatist struggles and Russian support for the Armenians, much of the region is under Armenian control. South Ossetia and Abkhazia are separatist regions of Georgia, both of which have seen violent clashes with government forces. Russia has supported Abkhazia, which now enjoys de facto independence.

22 See I. Yelistratov, *Izvestia*, April 27, 1991, p. 1, as translated in *Current Digest of the Soviet Press*, May 29, 1991.

23 Most of these refugees have still not returned to their original homes. On casualties here and in the North Caucasus, see Vladimir Mukomel, "Vooruzhennye mezhanotsional'nye konflikty: ludskie poteri, ekonomicheskii ushcherb i sotsial'nye posledstivia," in Martha Brill Olcott, Valery Tishkov, and Aleksei Malashenko, eds., *Identichnost' i konflikt v postsovetskikh gosudarstvakh* (Moscow: Carnegie Moscow Center, 1997).

24 The previous hierarchical formulation was "nations," "national communities," and "national groups" in declining order of importance.

25 The final document reflects the work of three ministers of nationality affairs: Valery Tishkov, Sergei Shakhrai, and Viacheslav Mikhailov.

26 See Hurst Hannum, "Rethinking Self-Determination," *Virginia Journal of International Law*, vol. 34, no. 1, Fall 1993, pp. 1–69.

27 On ethnic federalism and its limits see, Vojislav Stanovic, "Problems and Options in Institutionalizing Ethnic Relations," *International Political Science Review*, vol. 13, no. 4, 1992, pp. 359–79.

28 The most comprehensive collection of treaties and agreements between Moscow and the various subjects of the federation is Mikhail N. Guboglo, ed., *Federalism vlasti i vlast' federalizma* (Moscow: Inteltex, 1997).

29 According to its 1978 constitution, Spain is a parliamentary monarchy consisting of nineteen centrally recognized autonomous regions, each headed by a president of the government.

30 Leokadia M. Drobizheva et al., *Demokratizatsiya i obrazy natsionaliszma v Rossiiskoi Federatsii 90-kh godov* (Moscow: Mysl, 1996).

31 B. O'Leary and J. McGarry, "Regulating Nations and Ethnic Communities," in Albert Breton, Gianluigi Galeotti, Pierre Salmon, and Ronald Wintrobe, eds., *Nationalism and Rationality* (New York: Cambridge University Press, 1995).

32 For a discussion of the ongoing debates, see Valery Tishkov, "Natsional'nosti i passport," *Izvestia*, November 4, 1977.

33 See L. M. Drobizheva, A. R. Aklaev, V. V. Koroteeva, and G. U. Soldatova, *Demokratizatsiya i Obrazy Natsionalizma v Rossiikoi Federatsii 90-kh Godov* (Moscow: Mysl, 1996); L. M. Drobizheva, ed., *Sotsial'naya i Kul'turnaya Distantsii. Opyt Mnogonatsional'noi Rossii* (Moscow: Institute of Sociology, 1998).

34 See Mikhail N. Guboglo, *Razvivaiuschiisya elektorat Rossii* (Moscow: Institute of Ethnology and Anthropology, 1996).

35 See Valery Tishkov, "Political Anthropology of the Chechen War," *Security Dialogue*, vol. 28, no. 4, December 1997, pp. 425–37.

4
Economic Reform versus Rent Seeking

Anders Åslund and Mikhail Dmitriev

On August 17, 1998, Russia faced financial collapse. The government devalued the ruble, defaulted on its domestic treasury bills, and proclaimed a 90-day moratorium on its foreign debt payments. The ruble exchange rate quickly fell to one-third of its prior value. Within a week President Boris Yeltsin dismissed the reformist government headed by Sergei Kiriyenko, in effect for failing to secure Duma approval of measures that might have prevented the crisis. In the month of September, inflation rose to 38 percent per month, contributing to an annual inflation rate of 84 percent in 1998. The bank and payments system collapsed. As a result, the Russian gross domestic product (GDP) fell by 4.6 percent in 1998 (with a similar contraction expected in 1999). As of the end of 1998, Russia's GDP had fallen by almost half since 1990.

The severity of Russia's economic problems, and the seeming inability of a succession of governments to solve them, have raised numerous questions about the painful reforms Russia's people have endured since the collapse of communism. This chapter examines the main factors behind Russia's economic development since the end of the Soviet Union. It begins with a brief review of key events from the Soviet period that influenced the initial transition, then considers the successes and failures of the reformist government in 1992 and 1993. In 1994 and 1995, the government was no longer a reformist one, but it did complete the first macroeconomic stabilization and large-scale privatization. In 1996–1998, reform ideas were again much discussed, and some were even attempted, but their accomplishments fell short of their goals. In August 1998 financial disaster struck.

The August 1998 crisis caused great turmoil in Russia and hurt the welfare of its people badly. It is possible that the crisis will stimulate more realistic economic and political thinking, but in truth the main shortcomings of Russia's economic policy have long been known. A fundamental problem is that the Russian government has never achieved a fiscal balance. On the one hand, state revenues are declining because of an ineffective and widely ignored tax system. On the other hand, the government has failed to reduce and rationalize government expenditures. As a result of a lasting and large budget deficit, short-term government debts accumulated to a level that Russia's creditors no longer considered sustainable. The state debt service became excessive not primarily because of the size of the debt, but because of high interest rates caused by a badly functioning capital market.

Economically, the solution to Russia's problem was obvious. For years, the government and international financial institutions had made reasonable proposals to simplify the tax system, to broaden its base by abolishing exemptions, and to reduce the top tax rates. Other areas where there was general agreement on at least the broad contours of needed reforms included curbing abusive government interference; protecting property rights, including the private ownership of land; subjecting natural monopolies to market regulation; reinforcing the rule of law; and improving the social safety net.

The adoption of these and other widely discussed measures could have saved the Russian people a great deal of suffering. The key question is why hardly any of them were undertaken. Our answer is that the rent-seeking interests in Russian society were so strong that they overpowered concern for the common good.[1] Moreover, the competition among the rent seekers was so fierce that they could not halt their behavior but drove themselves to financial collapse.

By *rent seeking* we mean the attempt to make money from the government, either directly through state subsidies or indirectly through government regulations.[2] For much of the period since 1991, the history of economic reform in Russia can be best understood as a struggle between reformers trying to create a normal market economy and rent seekers trying to make money on market distortions. We focus in this chapter on what the most important forms of rent seeking were, and how and why they evolved. In our conclusion, we comment upon three aspects of the Russian transition: the design of the reforms, the efficacy of international assistance, and the politics of economic reform.

ECONOMIC ASPECTS OF THE SOVIET COLLAPSE

The demise of the Soviet Union had multiple causes, but serious economic imbalances and distortions were certainly among the most important of them. Soviet finances collapsed in 1991, as the union republics stopped sending tax revenues to Moscow. The Soviet government faced a huge budget deficit, but international financing dried up when the Soviet Union was no longer able to service its foreign debt. In late 1991 the central government lived on little more than the emission of money. To make matters worse, the union republics started issuing their own ruble credits without any coordination with the Soviet State Bank: the more money any republic issued, the larger share of the common Soviet GDP it obtained.

This huge issue of credit would have caused hyperinflation had not most prices remained state controlled. Instead, inflationary pressures took the form of devastating shortages of nearly all goods. In the fall of 1991 food stores were typically empty, and whenever goods were delivered, long lines of customers appeared. For most workers it made little sense to earn money when one then had to spend hours queuing to use it. The idiosyncratic regulation of most prices led to incredible distortions: commodity prices were extremely low, often less than 1 percent of world prices, while industrial consumer goods were grossly overpriced.

The foreign trade regime aggravated these economic distortions. The Soviet Union essentially had a special exchange rate for every major good, and the differences between these rates were large. During the period of President Mikhail Gorbachev's partial economic reforms, the number of Soviet enterprises with the right to engage in foreign trade skyrocketed from 213 in 1988 to almost 20,000 in 1990.[3] With the right connections, these enterprises could acquire oil or metals at low Soviet state prices, obtain export licenses and quotas from foreign trade authorities, and sell the commodities abroad at the much higher world prices.

The Law on Cooperatives of May 1988 had made it legal to establish freely operating private enterprises, but the rest of the economy remained highly regulated. Many private trading cooperatives were set up by state enterprise managers together with politicians, state officials, and shrewd businessmen. One technique they favored was to buy commodities at low controlled prices from the state enterprises they managed and to sell them at market prices for private gain. Commercial banks became the most prominent new freewheeling cooperatives.

The so-called red directors—state enterprise managers who flourished in the midst of the economic crisis because of inconsistent state regulations—belonged to the old communist elite, but their behavior was copied by new bankers, traders, and others. As Michael Dobbs put it:

> There was a *fin de régime* atmosphere in Moscow in the spring of 1991, and bureaucrats were lining up to jump ship before it was too late.... Many members of the elite were now discovering that they could maintain their privileged positions in society even without ideology.... Why drive a Volga when you could be driving a Mercedes?[4]

In effect, the economic *nomenklatura* opted out of the socialist system for a partial market economy, leaving the Soviet elite split and politically vulnerable. This extraction of resources from the socialist economy virtually guaranteed the breakdown of the Soviet economic system. Ordinary Russians noticed who in the old elite had stood up against the Soviet system: since the red directors ensured the collapse of the Soviet Union, they were widely perceived as sensible heroes who understood that a market economy was necessary.[5]

But while these early proponents of a partial market economy had become quite rich, they still wanted more. They were prepared to fight for their privileges using their connections and fortunes— but not for a liberal market economy with real competition. Gravediggers of the old Soviet system, these rent seekers were also the harshest enemies of radical reforms aimed at establishing a level playing field.

Russia at the end of communism has often been described as an institutional vacuum, but that is not quite true. Many institutional anomalies incompatible with a market economy lingered. Relative prices were enormously distorted; multiple and highly varied exchange rates persisted; monetary emission was virtually uncon-strained; interest rates were set at low nominal levels in spite of rising inflation; entrepreneurship was subject to rigorous licensing; myriad regulations persisted on the books. Ironically, little in the economy was free except for banking. The government no longer owned or controlled everything, but real private property rights had yet to emerge. State enterprise managers tended to pilfer whatever public property they could. And most political institutions were too weak to stop them.

AN ATTEMPT AT RADICAL ECONOMIC REFORM, 1991–1993

In a speech to the Russian Congress of People's Deputies on October 28, 1991, President Boris Yeltsin announced his intention to move the country from the Soviet economic system toward a market economy. Yeltsin's main proposals were adopted as a guideline for the govern-ment's economic policies by an overwhelming majority of the depu-ties a few days later. One week after that, Yeltsin abolished the old Soviet branch ministries and appointed a new type of government with an economic reform team headed by liberal economist Yegor Gaidar. Yeltsin, Gaidar, and the young liberals who now led many ministries made no secret of their intention to build a Western-style market economy in Russia as fast as possible.[6]

Although the communists were discredited after the abortive hard-line coup in August 1991, the young reformers encountered vicious criticism from the outset. Even before the reforms had been launched, Vice President Aleksandr Rutskoi ridiculed the leading reform ministers as "small boys in pink shorts and yellow boots."

The reformers focused on getting state finances under control and drew up a balanced budget for the first quarter of 1992. Another priority was to liberalize prices, domestic and foreign trade, and entrepreneurship, but resistance to these changes was particularly fierce. Some of the arguments made against the reforms were pat-ently absurd. Rutskoi claimed, for example, that, "The liberalization of prices without the existence of a civilized market requires strict price control. . . . In all civilized countries such strict controls exist."[7] Behind such bizarre statements, however, lay the interests of the so-called industrialists—managers of large state firms. And few among the public had enough understanding of a real market economy to judge the accuracy of such statements.

The key to understanding this highly antagonistic period is the events of 1992—the year the rich and powerful made their big money. In the spring of 1992 the state price of oil was 1 percent of the world market price; the domestic prices of other commodities were about 10 percent of world prices. Managers of state companies bought oil, metals, and other commodities from the state enterprises they controlled on their private accounts, acquired export licenses and quotas from corrupt officials, arranged political protection for themselves, and then sold the commodities abroad at world prices. Their gains can be calculated easily by multiplying the average price differential by the volume of commodities exported and deducting export taxes. The total export rents were no less than $24 billion in the peak year of 1992, or 30 percent of GDP, since the exchange rate was very low that year. The resulting private revenues were accumulated abroad, which led to massive capital flight.

A second way to get rich was to borrow money from the Central Bank of Russia. In 1992 the bank gave enormous credits at subsidized rates of 10 percent or 25 percent a year (at a time when inflation was 2,500 percent a year). Viktor Gerashchenko, also the last chairman of the Soviet State Bank, gave bank credits as a favor to well-connected businessmen. In 1992 alone, the net credit issue of the Central Bank of Russia was 32 percent of GDP. Directed credits to enterprises amounted to 23 percent of GDP. While these benefits were less concentrated than export rents, they made Russia's bankers rich.

The bankers, for their part, argued that the credit issue was "Keynesian," that is, that it would expand demand and support industrial production. In fact, the bankers cared little when Russia's industrial production plummeted in the wake of hyperinflation caused by excessive credit issue. The reformers never managed to get control over the Central Bank of Russia. Georgy Matiukhin, Gerashchenko's predecessor as chairman, reported in his memoirs how he was ousted from the bank in June 1992 because he insisted on raising the absurdly low interest rates contrary to demands from Ruslan Khasbulatov, the speaker of the Supreme Soviet (the old semi-democratic Russian parliament).[8]

A third way of making a fortune in the transition period was through import subsidies. In the winter of 1991–1992, there was great fear both inside and outside Russia that the country would suffer famine. Under such a threat, the reformers could not abolish the existing import subsidies for food. The subsidies meant that an importer only had to pay 1 percent of the going exchange rate when he purchased essential foods. After importing them, he could sell the foods relatively freely on the domestic market and pocket the subsidy for himself. These imports were paid for with Western "humanitarian" export credits, which were added to Russia's state debt. The total value of the import subsidies was assessed at 17.5 percent of Russia's GDP in 1992 by the International Monetary Fund (IMF). These rents were highly concentrated among a limited number of traders in Moscow, operating through the old state agricultural monopoly companies.

The total gains from these three activities amounted to no less than 71 percent of GDP in 1992. (This is a gross number, so the net gains to several thousand people involved are significantly smaller, but the concentration of income was extreme, and the revenues were huge in 1991 and 1993 as well.) In a few short years, Russia went from having an income differentiation close to the European average to having one of much higher Latin American proportions.

Other rents, while significant and harmful, were much smaller. Direct state subsidies, mainly to agriculture, the coal industry, and large enterprises, for example, were 10.8 percent of GDP in 1992 (see Figure 1). Much has also been written about the economic impact of the Russian Mafia. If by Mafia one means "an industry which produces, promotes, and sells private protection,"[9] we can estimate revenues from racketeering by focusing on the retail trade, whose total sales amounted steadily to one-third of GDP. In 1992 a standard protection fee was said to be 20 percent, but not all businesses paid for protection. If we assume that the average protection revenues were 10 percent of total retail sales, the total annual revenues from protection would amount to 3 percent of GDP.[10] Moreover, protection is a comparatively labor intensive occupation, which means that net revenues per person must have been much less in racketeering than in the other rent-seeking activities mentioned above.

The rent seekers—state enterprise managers, bankers, corrupt officials, and commodity traders—were well organized and politically influential. Even so, after initial defeats the reform government made amazing headway. Gradually, price and export controls were eliminated, bringing Russian commodity prices closer to world prices. The dysfunctional ruble zone was broken up, and each of the former

FIGURE 1
Enterprise Subsidies, 1992–1997

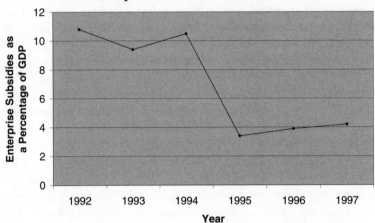

Sources: Goskomstat Rossii, *Rossiiskii statisticheskii yezhegodnik 1997* (Moscow: Goskomstat, 1997), pp. 304, 519, 520; Russian European Center for Economic Policy, *Russian Economic Trends*, vol. 7, no. 3 (1998), pp. 71–2.

Soviet republics established its own national currency by late 1993.[11] Subsidized credits were abolished in late September 1993 by government decree, and by November 1993 Russia had positive real interest rates. At the end of 1993 the exchange rate was fully unified, eliminating the last import subsidies. In parallel, the privatization of small enterprises was successfully undertaken, and large-scale privatization was under way. The economic and social costs of these changes were great, but in late 1993 the reformers had accomplished so much that the reforms appeared irreversible.

There are several explanations of why fundamental reforms that seemed impossible in the spring of 1992 were successfully undertaken in late 1993.[12] Several rents declined for reasons beyond the control of politics. First, as people and enterprises learned not to hold money in any form, the velocity of money rose, which reduced the inflation tax. Therefore, the budget deficit could no longer be financed with the emission of credits. Second, as the media exposed various forms of rent seeking and people learned more about how a market economy operates, the public grew much less tolerant of unjustified subsidies. Third, a majority of the Russian voters expressed support for radical economic reforms in a referendum in

April 1993. This gave the reformers a strong boost. And finally, the dissolution of the Congress of People's Deputies in September 1993 created a temporary political vacuum that offered reformers (but also the rent seekers) uncommon opportunities to advance their agenda.

At the same time, a number of developments went against the tide of reform. At the end of January 1992 President Yeltsin issued a decree declaring the complete freedom of domestic trade. Instantly, tens of thousands of Russians took to the streets in the big cities and started trading all sorts of goods at whatever prices they could command. They also threatened the interests of established traders with their effective competition. Alas, after only three months, Moscow's Mayor Yuri Luzhkov prohibited free street trading. Mayors of other big cities followed suit, and this brief interlude of free enterprise in Russia came to an end. In May 1993 reform foes acted on regional demands for comprehensive licensing of all firms, which further blocked the free development of enterprise.[13]

The political support for the reforms expressed in the April 1993 referendum did not endure. Russians had anticipated a large decline in economic output and consumption, but when a new round of inflation began, many attributed the primary blame to the reformers who had liberalized prices—not to those who had issued more money. The reformers suffered a severe setback in the parliamentary elections in December 1993, forcing the departure of reformist deputy prime ministers Yegor Gaidar and Boris Fedorov. Anatoly Chubais, a lone reformist, stayed on as deputy prime minister in charge of privatization.

Yet the red directors received an even worse blow in the elections. Their leading organization, the Russian Union of Industrialists and Entrepreneurs, had sponsored the political party Civic Union. Although the Civic Union was perceived as a leading political force in the second half of 1992, it received only 2 percent of the popular vote. The declining political power of the red directors was reflected in shrinking benefits given to them by the government.

LINGERING REFORMS BUT NO REFORM GOVERNMENT, 1994–1995

The exit of all the reformers except Chubais from the government led to a widespread expectation of significant reversals in the reform policies, but in fact there was little change in economic policy in 1994. Prime Minister Viktor Chernomyrdin wanted neither reform nor reversal. Inflation declined and privatization proceeded, but few institutional reforms were undertaken: leading ministers were primarily lobbying for privileges for their favorite enterprises.

The budget balance was gradually being undermined. On "Black Tuesday," October 11, 1994, the exchange rate of the ruble fell precipitously by 27 percent. By this time, the exchange rate had assumed a real economic meaning to many Russians. In response to a popular outcry against economic mismanagement, Yeltsin sacked his leading economic policy makers, apart from Chernomyrdin. At long last, central banker Gerashchenko was dismissed. Chubais was given the reins of macroeconomic policy as first deputy prime minister.

In 1995, for the first time, the Russian government and the Central Bank pursued a coordinated economic policy aimed at macroeconomic stabilization. The government halved the fiscal deficit to 5.4 percent of GDP, mainly by reducing all kinds of enterprise budgets in the consolidated state budget from 10.5 percent of GDP in 1994 to 3.4 percent of GDP in 1995 (see Figure 1). This was an extraordinary blow to a number of interest groups, reducing rent seeking to only 8 percent of GDP.

In the spring of 1995 Russia concluded a full-fledged standby agreement with the International Monetary Fund with substantial financing.[14] By the summer of 1996, financial stabilization had been attained. Inflation dropped to 22 percent in 1996 and to 11 percent in 1997.

Russian bankers were divided over the issue of stabilization. Until the summer of 1995, the Association of Russian Banks pressured the government and the Central Bank for subsidized credits. This, unfortunately, only led to continued high inflation. Opposing financial stabilization, the Association engineered the ouster of Tatyana Paramonova, acting chair of the Central Bank, in the summer of 1995. When the interbank market dried up in the fall of 1995, however, financially strong banks limited their trade to each other and excluded weak banks that they did not want to receive any state support. The strong banks benefited from the sale of cheap bank assets as one bank bankruptcy followed another. From 1991 until 1997, the Central Bank rescinded the licenses of more than 700 banks. The unity of the Association of Russian Banks had been broken.

The other big economic event of this period was the completion of the privatization of almost 18,000 large and medium-sized enterprises through vouchers. Officially, more than 70 percent of the economy—measured as a share of GDP—now belongs to the nonstate sector. Many complaints have been raised about privatization; a common one is that the old management has acquired too much ownership. Studies show, however, that only 18 percent of the shares of privatized large and medium-sized enterprises belonged to the old managers in 1996.[15] When one considers that the state managers practically owned public enterprises before privatization, the current situation should be seen as a considerable reduction in the extent of their ownership.

Another complaint is that enterprise restructuring was too limited. In fact, 33 percent of large and medium-size enterprises changed management between 1992 and 1996, and about 25 percent of Russia's large and medium-sized enterprises have gone through substantial enterprise restructuring.[16] In our view, the insecure status of private property rights (including land ownership) and excessive state regulation of the economy are much more responsible for current economic problems in Russia than imperfections in the privatization process. Local authorities continue to harass entrepreneurs with arbitrary taxation and numerous inspections, and businessmen still have limited legal recourse.

A third complaint is that privatization has led to a concentration of wealth. Almost all of Russia's biggest companies have been traded freely on an open stock market, and the total market capitalization has vacillated between 5 and 20 percent of GDP from 1996 to 1998. This means that the market value that state enterprise managers got from the voucher privatization of their enterprises was only between 1 and 4 percent of GDP in total, compared with 71 percent of GDP through export rents, import subsidies, and subsidized credits in 1992. Thus, the concentration of wealth was not caused by privatization but by other forms of rent seeking. The fact that the privatization process was comparatively transparent and visible undoubtedly contributed to public resentment of it: the average Russian generally overestimated the value of industrial plants, for example, while not realizing the huge volumes of money passing through financial markets. Nonetheless, the political consequences of this popular illusion are real—and harmful.

A fourth criticism concerns a special "loans-for-shares scheme" that was introduced in 1995 for the privatization of a limited number of very large enterprises. The movers behind this scheme were not red directors, but some new bankers, notably Vladimir Potanin of Oneximbank and Mikhail Khodorkovsky of Menatep. The government's dilemma was that too many large enterprises remained state-owned, even after the voucher privatization was completed in the summer of 1994, and it had proven difficult to sell enterprises for money in cash-strapped Russia. Stock prices were tiny in relation to asset values, and large sales of additional stocks would have further depressed stock prices. The idea arose to sell large blocks of state shares through open auctions; it was thought that this would not depress stock prices, although the offering prices would be current market prices. Unfortunately, the auctions became closed, and the offering prices almost equaled the closing prices. As a result, Oneximbank seized control of Norilsk Nickel, the huge metallurgical company, and Sidanko, an oil company. Menatep took over Yukos, the oil company; Boris Berezovsky of the Logovaz car dealership got the Sibneft oil company at a very low price.

The loans-for-shares scheme attracted great public criticism, even though only fifteen enterprises were sold and not all the loans-for-shares privatizations were profitable for the auction winners. Only the four deals mentioned above were really economically significant. And these privatizations hardly changed the system; they only transferred the benefits of management theft from some red directors to some new capitalists (and tarnished Chubais's reputation). When Oneximbank took over Sidanko, it announced that the prior management had siphoned off $350 million a year from the company. Presumably Oneximbank's top managers started doing the same. Still, the total cash flows that could be expropriated from these companies were well below half a percent of GDP.

The importance of the reforms between 1994 and 1995 should not be exaggerated. A government of industrial lobbies ruled. Prime Minister Chernomyrdin secured extraordinary benefits for his creation, the Gazprom natural gas monopoly, granting it extensive tax exemptions at the end of 1993 amounting to some 1–2 percent of GDP. First Deputy Prime Minister Oleg Soskovets secured tax exemptions for the metal industry amounting to about 2 percent of GDP. Soskovets also supported the National Sports Fund, which got the right to import alcohol and tobacco tax-free. The Fund soon became the leading importer of these goods to Russia. These benefits amounted to another 2 percent of GDP. The agrarian lobby successfully resisted the privatization of land and the deregulation of agriculture. The rent seekers had regrouped to seek new forms of rents, notably tax exemptions. Nonetheless, the size of these rents was far less than they had been in 1992–1993, and they were increasingly tax exemptions rather than government financing. As massive tax evasion prevailed and the tax system was arbitrary, however, it is not obvious what a normal tax payment should have been.

Although Anatoly Chubais was the only significant reformer left in the government, the reformers were publicly blamed for the ongoing economic decline, while those in the government who unabashedly lobbied for their private interests escaped unscathed. The parliamentary elections in December 1995 dealt another blow to the reformers. The communists reemerged as a serious political threat, mainly because the reformers were split into too many parties.[17] In January 1996 President Yeltsin sacked his last reformist minister with the oft-quoted words: "Chubais is guilty for everything."

THE STAGNATION OF REFORM, 1996–1998

As Russia entered 1996, a new fear of communist revenge dominated Russian politics. Most anticommunist forces joined hands to counter that threat. This offered a new position of privilege to the so-called oligarchs, essentially new businessmen who had benefited from the loans-for-shares deals. The elections highlighted the political importance of money and owner control over media. Media magnates Vladimir Gusinsky and Boris Berezovsky (who controlled the TV channels NTV and ORT, respectively) emerged as major political forces. And the election results confirmed that the new Russian businessmen had gained real political clout. One reflection of their new power was that the top bankers nominated Vladimir Potanin to be first deputy prime minister, and Berezovsky became deputy secretary of the Security Council. Both aroused such controversy that they were soon ousted: Potanin lasted about six months, Berezovsky, twelve months.

Nineteen hundred and ninety-six was a year of no reform. The government contained no significant reformer, and the political will to reform was missing. The government let the budget deficit rise to 8 percent of GDP in 1996, and the real yields of its treasury bills exceeded 100 percent a year before the presidential elections in June 1996, as the government tried to sell more than the market was prepared to buy. The treasury bill market became a source of rent seeking for bankers, since only some privileged people were allowed to buy treasury bills for much of 1996.

The restless Moscow elite soon became frustrated with a government that did nothing to resolve the country's mounting economic problems. In response to calls from a broad political spectrum for a new reform government, Yeltsin reappointed Chubais as first deputy prime minister in March 1997. Joining Chubais in the cabinet was Boris Nemtsov, the successful reformist governor of Nizhny Novgorod. Their reform offensive, however, ended abruptly in July 1997. The new businessmen were no more prepared to accept free markets than were the old red directors. In July 1997 Berezovsky and Gusinsky turned against the reformers in the government with a vengeance because they had initiated an open auction of Svyazinvest, the telecommunications holding company. The new capitalists were as committed to rent seeking as the old red directors had been; they demanded their due from the government as payback for supporting Yeltsin in the 1996 presidential elections. In October 1997 Berezovsky worked with the communists and Prime Minister Chernomyrdin to increase the budget deficit in an apparent attempt to undermine the reformers in government.

The Asian financial crisis started to hurt Russia in late October 1997. Since Russia had just decided to increase the budget deficit, the government failed to tighten its fiscal policy until February. By then, interest rates had again risen to more than 100 percent a year. Only in late March 1998 did Yeltsin sack his passive Prime Minister Chernomyrdin; one month later, he appointed a reformist government under Sergei Kiriyenko. By then, however, the crisis was so severe that even a government with sufficient parliamentary support—which Kiriyenko did not have—would have had difficulty carrying out the necessary reforms.

Russia's financial problems had been a long time in the making. For years, the country had maintained an excessively large budget deficit. Its fast-growing, short-term government debt could not be sustained. As creditors withdrew, interest rates rose repeatedly above 100 percent a year. And at the same time that Russia badly needed capital inflows, red tape and arbitrary taxation rendered its enterprise environment cumbersome, deterring both domestic and foreign direct investment.

In July 1998 the Russian government concluded an agreement with the IMF on significant and swift budget deficit reductions. Yet four major interest groups continued pushing their country toward the abyss. First, the big oil barons, including Boris Berezovsky, who wanted lower production costs, campaigned for a ruble devaluation, although they knew that this would lead to the bankruptcy of most banks and create other serious problems.[18]

Second, in July 1998 the Russian State Duma refused to accept a government proposal to move from a valued-added tax (VAT) based on actual payments to one based on an accrual basis. Had it been adopted, the change would have led to the taxation of barter, which is now exempt from Russian VAT taxation. Nor would the Duma agree to transfer some government revenues from the regions to the federal treasury. These two votes by the Duma were the real trigger of the ensuing financial collapse.

Third, the regional governors strongly resisted the transfer of any of their funding to the federal government. Regional revenues have held steady at about one and a half times as large as the federal revenues, and the regions spend slightly more than 2 percent of GDP on enterprise subsidies. Because these subsidies are disbursed by the governor in a discretionary fashion, they all but invite criminals to run for election as regional governors.

The fourth group that contributed indirectly to the financial collapse was the state bureaucracy, which doubled in size in the midst of economic crisis: an incredible 1.2 million bureaucrats (almost 2 percent of the labor force) were added from 1992 to 1998. The result is an extraordinary degree of bureaucratic interference in enterprises that deters investments and entrepreneurship.

It is easy to condemn the behavior of these groups as socially irresponsible, but in fact their actions were consistent with what their recent experiences had taught them: that the most ruthless and cunning rent seeker is the most successful; that the government was only bluffing when it warned of economic ruin; and that in an economic environment that changes all the time, one must seize all opportunities as soon as they appear.

The Russian economic crisis also had an important international dimension. The years 1996 and 1997 saw substantial foreign capital inflows into Russia, but these were almost entirely portfolio investments in stocks and bonds. Foreign portfolio investments skyrocketed from $8.9 billion in 1996 to $45.6 billion—or 10 percent of GDP—in 1997.[19] Foreign direct investment in 1997 was only $6.2 billion, and it fell to $2 billion in 1998. At the peak of the stock market in 1997, foreigners might have owned as much as 30 percent of the market capitalization of some $100 billion. The total stock of treasury bills in the summer of 1998 amounted to some $70 billion, of which foreigners held at least $25 billion.

All these inflows, however, actually encouraged capital flight of about $20 billion in each of the years 1996 to 1998, while capital outflows had subsided in 1994 and 1995. Rising capital outflows are a strong indication of increasing rents. Hence, the foreign portfolio investments contributed both to rent seeking and to the magnitude of the Russian financial crash. The loans to the Russian government diminished the need for the Russian state to collect taxes or to cut subsidies. The loans from the IMF and the World Bank were contingent on sound economic policies, but the contingency appears to have been ineffective, possibly because the much larger private portfolio investments were unconditional. Many Russian businessmen made big money by cheating foreigners or by seizing the assets of minority shareholders by any means possible (from transfer pricing to the straightforward seizure of assets to not servicing bond debts). Therefore, these inflows were counterproductive both to corporate governance and to reform. Opportunities for rent seeking appear to have dwindled after these inflows stopped in July 1998, but it is too early to tell whether this change represents a real adjustment on the part of government officials and Russian businessmen— or simply a lull while the rent seekers identify new opportunities.

STRATEGIC ECONOMIC PROBLEMS

The ultimate purpose of an economy is to produce economic growth, but Russia's economy has experienced significant contraction since 1990. While disputes over statistics make precise assertions difficult, the trendlines are quite clear: with the exception of 1997, the Russian GDP has fallen steadily for a decade. This steady decline can no

FIGURE 2
Growth in Gross Domestic Product, 1990–1998

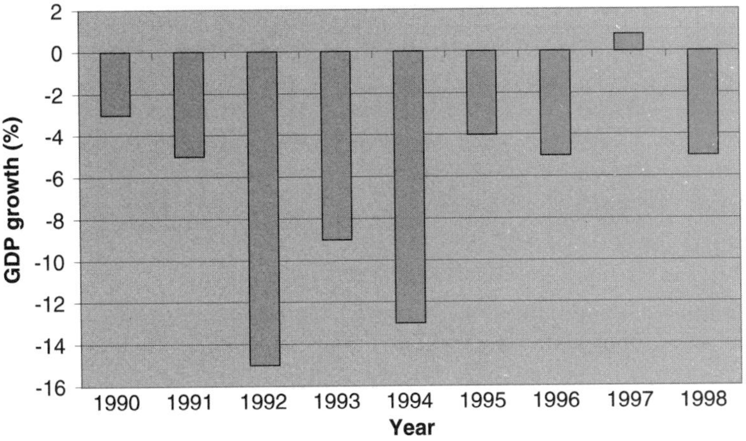

Source: *Russian Economic Trends*, no. 1 (1997), p. 94; Monthly Update, March 11, 1999, Table 1.

longer be blamed on temporary factors (see Figure 2), but on fundamental, long-term problems that ultimately brought about the financial crash of 1998.

First, while every viable state must obtain revenues to finance essential government activities, the Russian government for years has spent more than it has collected in taxes. The Russian tax system is inconsistent and arbitrary: tax collection absorbs much of the government's attention and hampers many productive activities, but in the end taxation provides little state financing. Second, the government has failed to control and rationalize its expenditures; it often does not pay (or is late in paying) its commitments, while large unjustified expenditures are disbursed. Third, markets of all kinds still function badly due to excessive regulation and the absence of the effective rule of law. This leads to high transaction costs, limited competition, and various financial and monetary problems.

These economic problems have one dominant cause: the fact that those who made substantial fortunes on inflation, regulations, subsidies, and other rents continue to oppose the effective development of a competitive market economy.[20] The state as the representative of a common public interest is weak; the state as a bureaucratic

TABLE 1
Russian Government Revenues as a Percentage of GDP, 1992–1998

	1992	1993	1994	1995	1996	1997	1998
Federal budget	15.6	13.7	11.8	12.2	13.0	11.6	10.6*
Regional budgets**	13.5	16.7	18.0	14.2	14.5	16.1	13.8*
Extrabudgetary funds**	10.9	8.6	9.1	7.6	7.7	9.1	9.9*
Total revenues	**38.3**	**36.8**	**34.7**	**31.9**	**32.1**	**33.0**	**32.8***

* Preliminary estimates
** Including transfers from federal budget

Source: Andrei Illarionov, "Kak byl organizovan rossiiskii finansovyi krizis," *Voprosy ekonomiki,* vol. 70, no. 11 (November 1998), p. 26.

impediment to productive economic activity is ubiquitous—a phenomenon Andrei Shleifer and Robert Vishny have termed "the grabbing hand."[21] The key question for the future is whether the Russian state can make the transition from stimulating rent seeking to encouraging profit seeking.

An Ineffective Tax System

The Russian tax system is an unfortunate combination of the old Soviet tax system, hasty and partial reforms from 1992, and subsequent changes of dubious legality often motivated by rent seeking—all enforced with large measures of inconsistency and sheer incompetence. While politically well-connected businessmen often escape taxation, many small entrepreneurs are forced out of business by confiscatory tax rates. Yet despite the high rates, the system collects little actual revenue.

Although declining tax revenues and growing budget deficits are the topics of frequent and alarmist news reports in Russia, total revenues have fallen only moderately—from 36.8 percent of GDP in 1993 to 32.8 percent in 1998—if one includes as government revenues the federal budget, all the regional budgets, and extrabudgetary funds like the pension fund (see Table 1). In 1997 Russia's total state revenues as a share of GDP were slightly larger than in the United States, but they were low by European standards, where the average is close to 50 percent of GDP. The average for other Commonwealth of Independent States countries, however, is slightly lower than in Russia, and it is the least reformist countries that maintain large state revenues.[22]

While Russia's formal tax rates do not appear to be excessively high, the country's tax laws do not define profits in the Western sense or permit deductions for many legitimate business expenses. Indexing taxes for inflation has also not been adopted. Taking inflation into account, the effective profit tax rate in Russia may have been as high as 77 percent in 1992 and 50 percent in 1994–1995.[23] The system is also quite complex: Russia has about 200 different taxes, most of which generate little revenue. Six main taxes account for about 75 percent of all revenues of the consolidated state budget.

Because the tax base is so narrow, a limited number of taxpayers pay huge taxes. Almost two-thirds of taxes are paid by industry, while only a tiny percentage of total revenues is collected directly from individuals.[24] The system suffers from a dangerous bias toward corporate taxation, especially taxation of manufacturing, and it discriminates against investment and production in favor of consumption. Even so, according to estimates by U.S. Treasury officials, an estimated 50 percent of the total VAT was not even collected in 1996, due to numerous exemptions, reduced rates, and lax enforcement. Tax exemptions are granted more on the basis of political and personal connections than for reasons of public policy. Individual income taxes and property taxes are still collected primarily through enterprises, as they were in the communist era. The system offers taxpayers little or no incentive to pay taxes; the risk of penalties hardly changes whether one pays taxes or not.

In the post-Soviet states, lower state revenues seem to be clearly correlated with faster recovery in GDP. The post-Soviet state is such a monster of arbitrary intervention that it can only be controlled if its resources are severely reduced. To stimulate growth, a government must accept a moderate level of tax revenues—25 percent of GDP at most.[25] Subsidies need to be minimized to reduce harmful state intervention. Unfortunately, a statist approach has persisted in Russia, and the IMF has continuously supported this policy of high taxes and ruthless tax collection. In our view, Russia needs to cut

TABLE 2
Russia's State Expenditures and Budget Deficit as a Percentage of GDP, 1992–1998

	1992	1993	1994	1995	1996	1997	1998
Federal expenditures**	38.0	24.3	23.2	17.6	22.1	18.4	15.5*
Regional and local expenditures	12.0	16.1	17.5	14.5	14.8	16.9	14.7*
Extrabudgetary funds	8.4	8.0	8.6	7.6	7.7	9.0	9.4*
Total expenditures	56.7	45.6	45.1	37.6	41.5	40.5	38.1*
State budget deficit	18.4	9.4	10.4	5.7	9.4	7.5	5.3

* Preliminary estimates
** Including budgetary transfers

Sources: Andrei Illarionov, "Kak byl organizovan rossiiskii finansovyi krizis," *Voprosy ekonomiki*, vol. 70, no. 11 (November 1998), p. 26; Brunswick Warburg, *Russian Monthly*, Moscow, March 1999, p. 7.

taxes to boost production, in the expectation that economic growth will eventually reverse the temporary shortfall in tax revenues.

Excessive and Unjust Public Expenditures

Russia's public expenditures are large in comparison with other countries of the former Soviet Union, and Russia's budget deficit remains considerable (see Table 2). The huge state debt service is paid for by the federal government. Even so, regional and local budgets as well as extrabudgetary funds have expanded at the expense of federal expenditures in recent years.

During the period of high inflation (1992–1994), the Russian government (and the governments of many other transition economies) boosted social expenditures as a share of the GDP, but did not render them more efficient. During those three years, contrary to public perceptions, social spending increased by more than 5 percent of GDP. In parallel, expenditures of regional budgets, measured as a share of the GDP, also grew rapidly, mainly because of increased subsidies and social spending. As a result, in 1994 social expenditures, including subsidies for housing and public transport, exceeded

50 percent of general governmental expenditures (probably for the first time in Russia's history).[26]

Unfortunately, these increases did not mean that the funds were spent efficiently or fairly. By 1994 only 12 percent of all social transfers (excluding pensions) went to the poorest 20 percent of the Russian people.[27] By 1996 the wealthiest 30 percent of all households received no less than 70 percent of social transfers. Housing subsidies have held steady at 4 percent of GDP—almost one-quarter of all social spending—although they primarily benefit wealthy households with large apartments in cities.

Another concern is the prevalence of producer subsidies and non-targeted forms of social protection. A significant share of Employment Fund expenditures, for example, was used not for unemployment benefits but for enterprise subsidies. In 1995, according to officials with the Ministry of Labor and Social Affairs, approximately one-third of the resources of the Social Insurance Fund (contributions to the Social Insurance Fund amounted to 5.4 percent of the total wage bill) was allocated to so-called compulsory tourism—that is, hidden subsidies to a noncompetitive network of boarding houses, holiday resorts, and recreation centers inherited by Russia from the Soviet era.

While regressive transfers go to the wealthy and the large administrative bureaucracy works for its own advantage, a substantial share of the Russian population—38 percent in January 1999—lives below the poverty line. But even if they were not so inefficient or socially unjust, Russia's huge expenditures remain too large to be sustained.

Poorly Functioning Markets

The battle to liberalize the Russian economy has been a protracted one. Although prices and trade have been liberalized, state intervention remains both pervasive and arbitrary. The market does not yet function well. Russia ranks very low on several liberalization indices,[28] and corruption is pervasive. In the Heritage Foundation index, which comprises the largest number of countries, Russia ranks 106 among 160 countries in terms of economic freedom, while the Fraser Institute index puts Russia at 102 among 114 countries.[29] In the index of corruption perceptions compiled by Transparency International, Russia was reckoned to be the 10th most corrupt out of 85 countries in 1998.[30] Prices and markups are still high, the choice of goods is limited and their quality is not impressive, and regional price differentials are sizable. Particularly strong resistance to liberalization has come from the energy, agriculture, and foreign trade sectors. Yet even if competition is limited, there are no longer significant shortages of goods and services as there were in the Soviet past.

Most Westerners are struck by the degree of regulation persisting in Russia. Virtually all economic activities are subject to licensing, and multiple licenses are usually required. More than sixty state agencies inspect businesses, but instead of enforcing the strict regulations, state inspectors attempt to extort bribes. Much new legislation, particularly on environmental protection, seems more likely to offer new opportunities for bribe taking than for improving public policy. And the only recourse most businessmen have is to file an administrative complaint with the local authorities.

One consequence of the limited deregulation is that Russia has few enterprises and very few small enterprises.[31] The number of registered small private enterprises actually fell from 900,000 in 1994 to 810,000 in 1996. By 1997 the total number of legally registered enterprises had reached only 2.7 million, about one enterprise per fifty-five Russians. By contrast, the successful reform countries Poland and Hungary have already attained the normal Western ratio of one enterprise per ten people.[32] The paucity of enterprises is a result of a hostile enterprise environment that limits competition; it explains why Russia has attracted little foreign direct investment.

Russia also suffers from poorly functioning financial markets. Ordinary Russians do not trust banks (and for good reason), but keep most of their savings—an estimated $40 billion—in hard-currency cash. In August 1998 most Russian banks closed down at least temporarily, and many Russians who did have their savings in banks lost most of them. The Central Bank wants to eliminate more than 700 banks, almost half of the total. The banking crisis imposes additional fiscal pressures on the government, as some banks will have to be recapitalized to restore the payments system. Meanwhile the real sector (that is, the nonfinancial sector) of the economy suffers from a poor payments system, excessive financial risks, and a limited supply of credits, undermining the prospects for investment-driven economic recovery.

Recent historical experience in Central Europe indicates that a gap of 10 percent a year between banks' lending and borrowing rates is the norm immediately after stabilization.[33] In Russia, however, this gap has remained greater than 20 percent a year, even before the outbreak of the financial crisis in October 1997. It is likely to stay at about that level. The legal system is much weaker in Russia than elsewhere in Central Europe, making the collection of debts more cumbersome and expensive. Collateral is scarce, since little private property is held in the form of land. Information about borrowers is more scarce and less reliable in Russia than in Central Europe. Banking skills and the ability to assess creditworthiness are rare. And the crime rate is much higher in Russia than in Central Europe (the murder rate is as much as five to ten times higher). For all of these reasons, Russian banks demand larger margins—and they can do so because of the limited competition. Even so, the Russian banking industry has entered a period of depressed profits, consolidation, and bankruptcies.[34]

While the banks have big financial problems, the situation with business enterprises is hardly better. Financial discipline at the enterprise level is lax, and it is exacerbated by byzantine bankruptcy procedures, poor legal means to enforce creditor claims, and a weak court system. The results are mounting arrears of many kinds and the proliferation of payments in kind.

Monetization is low and it is not advancing. At the time of high inflation, it was natural that the monetization (measured as M2 in relation to GDP[35]) fell sharply from the high Soviet level of forced savings to barely 13 percent in 1993. It dropped further to about 10 percent in 1995, when the eventually successful stabilization attempt was launched (see Figure 3). The surprise is that the monetization has hardly risen after 1995, although inflation was brought under control. By comparison, in 1995 successful Central European reform countries such as Poland, Slovenia, and Hungary had a monetization with M2 amounting to 30–40 percent of GDP. Monetization in most post-Soviet countries, though, persists at about as low a level as in Russia.[36]

An explanation of the low level of monetization is that barter and various forms of nonmonetary forms of payments are expanding. The share of payments in Russian industry undertaken through barter rose from 6 percent of all sales in 1992 to 54 percent in August 1998, according to the Russian Economic Barometer, a regular poll of managers of Russian industrial enterprises (see Figure 4).[37]

FIGURE 3
Money Supply (M2) in Relation to GDP, 1990–1997

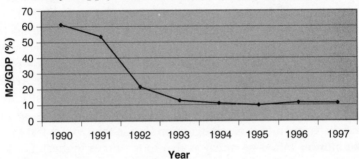

Note: Ruble M2 in mid-year; GDP measured in current prices.
Sources: Andrei N. Illarionov, "Inflyatsiya—denezhnoe yavlenie," *Voprosy ekonomiki*, vol. 69, no. 12 (December 1997), pp. 149–153; Russian European Center for Economic Policy, *Russian Economic Trends*, Monthly Update, July 2, 1998; authors' calculations.

FIGURE 4
Barter Payments in Sales of Industrial Enterprises, 1992–1998

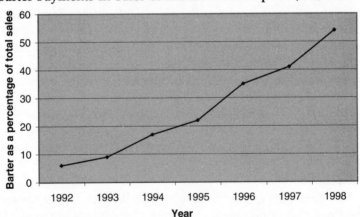

Source: S. Aukutsionek "Barter v rossiiskoi promyshlennosti," *Voprosy ekonomiki*, vol. 70, no. 2 (February 1998), pp. 51–60.

At the same time, plenty of money surrogates have emerged, so that only one-quarter of interenterprise transactions are conducted with money. The most common form of money surrogates are so-called offsets, which function like this: If an enterprise has not paid its taxes, it offers the government some products or services instead. If the government accepts, the tax delinquent has in effect extracted a government contract by not paying taxes. Moreover, through an offset an enterprise can avoid competition and boost its prices.

The standard communist explanation of why barter is so prevalent is that the economy suffers from a shortage of money. The typical suggested remedy is additional emissions of currency—but this confuses supply with demand. There is little demand for money because many enterprises prefer barter and money surrogates to payments in cash, while other businesses are too weak to demand payment in money. If the supply of money increased while the demand remained low, the result would only be inflation.

The standard Western explanation of barter is that it and other forms of noncash payments are motivated by tax avoidance, which seems supported by polls among businessmen.[38] Russia's value-added tax (VAT), in particular, is based on payments, not on invoices or deliveries on an accrual basis (as is typical in the West). Hence, companies that receive little or no payments in money are exempt from most of their potential VAT burden. For the Russian government and the IMF, one of the most important reforms that could be adopted would be to assess VAT on an accrual basis to reduce the incentives to barter in the current tax code.

Yet tax avoidance is not the whole explanation of the prevalence of barter. The same polls showed that 40 percent of the barter trade was perceived as involuntary. Typically, larger industrial enterprises compel smaller firms to accept payment in products they do not want.[39] Barter is most common among large enterprises producing intermediary industrial goods that can be sold easily—construction materials and metals, for example. It is clear that these manufacturers have chosen barter partly because it distorts prices and changes relative prices.

Clifford Gaddy and Barry Ickes have pointed out that the noncash economy is growing, not shrinking. The system is well-entrenched, with strong incentives for many to maintain it. The noncash economy is beneficial both to value-detracting and to raw-material producing companies, while the household sector loses in consumption and the government loses real tax revenues.[40] The essence of the post-Soviet noncash economy is the reluctance of large enterprises to adjust to market conditions at the expense of consumers (who get shoddy goods), the government (which cannot collect taxes), and politically weaker enterprises (which do not get paid in money). A transparent and competitive monetized economy offers no particular advantages for large enterprises. By contrast, relations with high government officials are crucial for an enterprise's success in a non-cash economy, and large enterprises typically have greater access to senior state officials.

A good example of this phenomenon is Gazprom, the natural gas monopoly that is Russia's biggest and richest company. Gazprom receives payment in money for only one-tenth of its domestic deliveries, although the firm clearly has the clout to demand more. Because Gazprom produces more natural gas than it can sell on an ordinary market and has minimal marginal costs, the firm uses barter to facilitate price discrimination and discounts. Gazprom's close links to the government also allow it to leverage larger and more secure benefits than it probably could earn in a competitive market.

Offsets are by their nature discretionary negotiations between big businessmen and government officials about large amounts of money, a process naturally imbued with corruption. Regional governments appear to be most corrupt, accepting 60 percent of taxes in money surrogates. Local governments might not have much clout against big companies, but even so they only accepted 43 percent of their revenues in money surrogates in 1996, suggesting they tried hard to get real money.[41] The federal government received about 25 percent of its revenues in offsets, which is an indication that the federal government is less corrupt than regional governments.[42] Money surrogates also comprise a substantial part of the regional and local expenditures—no less than 39 percent in 1996.[43] Thus, money surrogates not only distort prices and tax revenues but also divert public expenditures away from social spending toward public-works projects and enterprise subsidies.

Barter is also an important mechanism of management theft. In the spring of 1998, coal miners staged large strikes to demand that the government pay them months of back wages. But many of the mines in which these miners worked had already been privatized, and the government had already paid subsidies to the mines. Investigations showed that the mines received only two-thirds of the price their customers paid for the coal. The remaining one-third disappeared into the pockets of middlemen connected with some mine managers, who cheated both their own workers and other mine owners. As a result of the subsidization of the coal industry, it has become not only inefficient but thoroughly criminalized.[44]

Thus, in almost every respect, the ongoing barterization of the Russian economy represents a serious regression. It implies demonetization, tax evasion, and the rule of big, old enterprises over small, new enterprises. Both workers and shareowners suffer from its consequences: the only winners are a small group of big enterprise managers. By avoiding money payments, they reassure themselves that their personal relations with government officials and each other remain decisive. Thus, barter and money surrogates conserve the power structure in industry as well as the production structure. Little modernization and restructuring are likely in this environment.

WHERE IS RUSSIA GOING?

The Russian economy has gone through a decade of economic contraction. Economic policy is characterized by a duality: on the one hand, Russia wants to catch up with the developed world by embracing a liberal reform agenda. On the other hand, strong rent-seeking interests oppose reforms that would eliminate their particular advantages based on connections to power. Ironically, even as the role of the state is declining, the efforts of rent seekers to make money on the state effectively give the government less to redistribute, reducing rents more than output.

The current degree of government intervention in Russia is extraordinary by any international standard, and it is not likely to be sustained. Therefore, the government administration will have to be cut, as has happened in most other post-Soviet states. The degree of effective regulation will fall accordingly.

Similarly, the Russian government cannot continue to spend considerably more than it collects in taxes. Sooner or later the government must undertake a fundamental tax reform. A broad public consensus favors a fundamental tax reform leading to a system with a limited number of broad-based taxes with low tax rates of 20 percent or less. Similar tax reforms have been adopted in other former Soviet republics, such as Estonia, Georgia, Kazakhstan, and Kyrgyzstan.[45] In July 1998, after years of discussion, the State Duma incorporated many of these ideas in a new tax code. Even the Primakov government proceeded with the reduction of tax rates.[46]

Whatever happens with tax reform, state revenues are likely to decline in the short term. After the 1998 financial collapse, however, Russia has hardly any access to financing. It may get some additional loans from international financial institutions, additional privatization, or the refinancing of debt service, but selling Russian government bonds will be difficult for years to come. Even the inflation tax cannot reap much revenue because of the limited monetization. The key problem will be reducing the budget deficit at a time of declining state revenues. The Russian government will be forced to reduce sharply its expenditures, including those for state administration, enterprise and housing subsidies, and various *nomenklatura* benefits. In most of the post-Soviet states that have already done all this, the shrinking of government expenditures makes rent seeking less attractive. As the economy becomes more transparent, the incentives for entrepreneurship and profit seeking grow.

But is this politically feasible—or will the beneficiaries of the partial early reforms continue to block the necessary next steps? The key determinant for Russia's future is how rent seeking will evolve.[47]

The peak of rent seeking occurred in 1992, when the main rents were subsidized credits to enterprises (23 percent of GDP), export rents (30 percent), import subsidies (17.5 percent), and direct budget subsidies (10.8 percent), for a total of 81 percent of GDP.

By 1995 rents had plummeted. Subsidized credits and import subsidies were gone in 1994, when export rents contracted to about 3.7 percent of GDP.[48] Enterprise subsidies fell sharply in 1995 to 3.4 percent of GDP (see Figure 1). We may include 0.5 percent of GDP in rents from the loans-for-shares privatizations. Still, the narrow rents we focus on amounted to only about 8 percent of GDP.

Export rents continued falling, but they might still have been 2 percent of GDP in 1997. Enterprise subsidies recovered slightly to 4.2 percent of GDP in 1997. Here, however, we need to include foreign portfolio investments in our definition of rent seeking, since they were in effect free money, appropriated by ruthless businessmen as a consequence of a poor legal order or government inaction.

FIGURE 5
Rent Seeking, 1991–1998

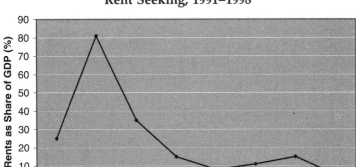

Source: authors' calculations.

We include enterprise bonds (about 2 percent of GDP in 1997), stock investments (about 4 percent), and excessive returns on treasury bills (about 3 percent). Thus, these amounted to 15 percent of GDP in rents in 1997—almost a doubling of the rents from 1995, although our calculations do not include tax exemptions, the benefits of authorized banks, and gains from barter and nonpayments.

The financial crisis of August 1998 eliminated the rents related to foreign financing, as well as the excessive returns on treasury bills. The only remaining rents are enterprise subsidies and some refinancing of banks—less than half a percent of GDP. Hence, the financial crisis seems to have cleaned out many rents and possibly prepared the ground for a low-rent economy. Figure 5 presents an approximation of the development of rents in Russia in the 1990s.

The sharp reduction of rents means much less money can be spent buying politicians and officials, reducing the incentives to distort economic policy to the benefit of rent seeking. The forces for rent seeking are also being dissipated: the red directors, for example, were a dominant political force as late as 1993, but they have now been partly replaced by or merged with Russia's new big capitalists. The capitalists are split themselves: a few top businessmen can reap private gains from discretionary state intervention, but most of them demand lower taxes and more freedom, plus the protection of a well-functioning legal system. Even the leading rent seekers have fought each other since July 1997. They suffered badly from the financial collapse of August 1998. No longer able to extract large rents, they have that much less available to corrupt government officials and politicians.

The regional governors appear to be the greatest remaining hurdle to a normal market economy. In recent years the regions have steadily gained authority at the expense of the federal government. As automatic members of the Federation Council (the upper house of the Russian parliament), regional governors have a final say in Russian legislation. Their power is reflected in the relative increase in the budgetary resources and decisions controlled by them. As regional budgets account for two-thirds of the revenues of the consolidated state budget, Russia has become the most decentralized federation in the world.[49] Regional governments are likely to be much less constrained by declining revenues than the federal government.

The powerful regional governors oppose a large and intrusive federal government, but they do value federal transfers—as well as their own power to intervene in the economy, and their regional regulations disrupt the unified Russian market. Federal government transfers to the regions have been quite small, peaking at 3.4 percent of GDP in 1994 and then declining.[50] Most regions are net recipients. Ironically, transfers tend to go to the regions that voted against the government in both the 1993 and 1995 elections—not to the regions with the greatest social need—thus showing that these transfers reflect the weakness of the federal government.[51] The regional transfers are not likely to increase as a share of GDP because of the falling federal tax revenues, but the regional governors nonetheless defend them forcefully.

To date the regional governors have been notorious for controlling certain prices, licensing and subsidizing enterprises, allocating administrative credits provided by regional banks, controlling exports from their regions, and generously subsidizing housing, utilities, and transportation. Fortunately, some of these practices have stopped. But regional governors are eager to control the licensing of all private enterprises and to mandate inspections of them by multiple local authorities—both to generate bribes and to intimidate entrepreneurs. The federal authorities could possibly impose a far-reaching deregulation from the center, but many argue that the federal government lacks the power to do this in the short run.

Another concern is that no less than 60 percent of all taxes at the regional level are being paid in nonmonetary forms, typically in offsets.[52] An enterprise that offers to provide goods or services instead of paying its taxes is in effect asking for a public contract without competing for it. These practices breed further corruption, making the regional governments appear more corrupt than the more constrained federal government.

In summary, the increased political weight of the regional governors is likely to limit state expenditures as a share of GDP. A reduction of the revenues of regional budgets as a share of GDP, however, is necessary to persuade regional authorities to reduce subsidies and to improve the targeting of social benefits. For the time being, regional governments are likely to remain far too intrusive in enterprises. After the so-called oligarchs have been cut down to size, the regional governors appear to be the main impediment to successful reforms.

CONCLUSION

In Russia today, all the standard features of the communist command economy are gone. The government no longer determines who manages enterprises; what they produce, sell, or buy; or what prices they set. A pluralist structure of ownership has been established. From early 1996 until the summer of 1998, Russia had a reasonably stable currency. Since the summer of 1998, however, Russia has been in a serious financial crisis. Despite many improvements over what existed before, the emerging Russian market economy still displays serious imperfections. State ownership is more extensive than in almost any Western state, and even fully privately owned enterprises are heavily dependent on the state. State power is exercised with more arbitrariness than would be accepted in the West, and businessmen have little legal recourse in their relations with the state.

The main themes of the Russian reform agenda have been deregulation, stabilization, and privatization. Unfortunately, nothing conclusive can be said about the design of the reforms, since so little was actually implemented. Deregulation of all kinds is essential to end rent seeking. The reformers fought for the liberalization of commodity prices, but they lost. As the domestic commodity prices were kept artificially low, exports could not be liberalized. The fear of starvation in the winter of 1991–1992 made it politically impossible to unify the exchange rate, which would have eliminated import subsidies. The reformers tried to liberalize domestic trade but with limited success. Gaidar pushed for considerable freedom for enterprises, but his efforts were rebuked. The preceding bizarre freedom of private banks persisted.

On fiscal policy, the reformers started out well, opting for a balanced budget in early 1992. Various quasi-fiscal expenditures, however, such as subsidized credits and import subsidies, became the dominant fiscal problems, with the Central Bank as the main culprit. Only after two years did the Ministry of Finance acquire elementary control over state expenditures. The Central Bank was independent of the government, but it was not interested in monetary stability, and it bred macroeconomic disaster.

One of the greatest misperceptions of the Russian transition is that privatization was the primary means by which personal enrichment occurred. Contrary to the common understanding, Russian enterprise ownership is reasonably well distributed, but it has not become effective ownership. Privatization is no alternative to deregulation, though it might facilitate deregulation in the future. Nor has privatization been an effective impediment to rent seeking. In the financial crisis of 1998, the Russian tycoons did not behave like capitalists who cared about the value of their property, but like rent seekers who thought only of the short-term cash flow.

After the government failed to establish the main pillars of a sound economic policy, little else succeeded. In the first years of transition social expenditure rose sharply as a share of GDP, and even now social transfers remain much too large. Russia's social expenditures still benefit the old *nomenklatura* more than they provide any social safety net for the needy. With populist demagogy, the old establishment has even boosted the regressiveness of Russia's social transfers.

In Russia, "industrial policy" has been a code word for demands for subsidies. Three industries have secured the most: the coal industry, agriculture, and the military-industrial complex. As a result, trade in their products has become criminalized, because subsidies are not only an indicator of rent seeking but also a strong inducement to organized crime.

There has been considerable international involvement in Russia's economic reforms. The IMF has been the dominant force for several reasons. Its main mission is to promote macroeconomic stabilization, which was new Russia's most pressing problem. The IMF also has a lot of money to offer for concrete programs; its narrow agenda provides for a clear focus; and it has been more active than other international actors. The IMF's finest achievement was the standby agreement in the spring of 1995 that led to stabilization, mainly due to a cut in enterprise subsidies of no less than 7 percent of GDP (see Figure 1). It was a highly daring action, as it occurred just before parliamentary and presidential elections, and the only real guarantor was Anatoly Chubais, first deputy prime minister. The IMF and the World Bank were important forces behind the deregulation of foreign trade, which eliminated most foreign trade rents.

The worst failure of the West was a sin of omission: not to support the stabilization program in early 1992. If the West had sponsored an IMF-like program then, it would have been possible to liberalize commodity prices and exports, to unify the exchange rate, and to introduce market interest rates from the beginning of 1992. The main blame for missing this window of opportunity belongs to the U.S. administration, the decisive Western policy maker at the time. The IMF, however, was guilty of advocating the maintenance of the ruble zone in spite of the fact that fifteen mutually independent central banks were all competitively emitting the same currency.

In the spring of 1996 the IMF concluded a three-year loan program called an Extended Fund Facility (EFF) with Russia. The formal conditions were reasonably firm, but the country was heading toward a budget deficit of more than 8 percent of GDP and sold treasury bills at interest rates of as much as 150 percent a year in real terms. This was a political rather than an economic decision, intended to save President Yeltsin in the presidential elections of June 1996. Saved he was, but at the expense of sound economic policy. The EFF agreement set the stage for Russia's ensuing boom and bust. The soft IMF approach convinced foreigners and Russians alike that Russia was too big—or too nuclear—to be allowed to fail. The EFF signaled that in Russia anything is allowed.

As of the spring of 1999, it is still early to judge whether the IMF program of July 1998 was too small, too late, or never feasible. Yet, in retrospect, it is difficult to believe that the IMF could ever have had a decisive impact in Russia after April 1, 1992—and no other international organization came close to matching its efforts.

A broader issue is the politics of reform, which is primarily a drawn-out struggle between reformers and rent seekers. Most advice given to reform governments tends to disregard how constrained their feasible choices really are, given the influence of powerful, rent-seeking interests. A common fallacy is that technical assistance will teach bureaucrats do their jobs, when the real problem is that many bureaucrats are corrupt and have no interest in seeing their powers or revenues reduced. Nor is it realistic to believe that a parliament that opposes private ownership will enact appropriate protections thereof.

Reformers face many important choices, particularly at the outset of reform. Before democratic governance has taken form, reformers must act quickly and decisively from above, as President Yeltsin did after he effectively assumed power in the fall of 1991. In November 1991 Yeltsin formed a government that swiftly formulated a reform program. He pronounced this program in a presidential speech to parliament, which voted to accept it. The missing element was international financial support, since the West was preoccupied with securing the Soviet debt, and was seemingly disinterested in Russia's future. Soon rent seekers got the upper hand in domestic politics.

Compared with Poland, the Czech Republic, and the Baltic states, all of which also launched radical reforms but received timely Western financial support, Russia looks like a failure. Compared with Ukraine, which did not try early reforms, however, Russia looks more successful. The reformers' failure was their inability to mobilize the popular majority that supported radical economic reform during the first year and a half of economic transition through early parliamentary elections.

In the second period of reform (1994–1995), the reformers could do little. In hindsight, the large-scale privatization hardly looks so important that it warranted the presence of a key reformer such as Chubais in the government. The stabilization of 1995–1996 appears less significant today, since it was not sustained but led to a new bout of rent seeking. Presumably, the reformers would have been better off politically had they declined to serve in a deeply corrupt government.

In 1997–1998, several prominent reformers held high government offices, but their reform proposals were obstructed by entrenched rent seekers. That this would be the outcome was not obvious at the outset; after all, Chubais had successfully stabilized the economy in 1995 with less political support. But the reformers themselves are ambiguous in their views on government service and international financial support. Boris Fedorov, for example, tends to argue that IMF support is harmful when he is not in government—but favors it as a lever against opponents when he is.

Russian reformers are learning to understand the new rent seekers' mode of operation, which makes their approach more political and less economic, and their political understanding is developing. Repeated failures of reformers in coalition governments to implement reforms successfully made many doubt the efficacy of reform from above at the current stage of development. And a growing reformist opinion argues that a parliamentary majority in favor of reform is necessary for real market economic reform. Russia is facing a regional conundrum, and no clear understanding about how to deal with the regions has arisen, making it unlikely that a solution will soon be found.

NOTES

[1] Joel S. Hellman, "Winners Take All: The Politics of Partial Reform in Postcommunist Transitions," *World Politics*, vol. 50 (January 1998), pp. 203–34.

[2] In principle, rent seeking could also include social transfers and public wages, but here we limit the discussion to rents extracted by businesses.

[3] Anders Åslund, *Gorbachev's Struggle for Economic Reform*, 2nd ed. (Ithaca: Cornell University Press, 1991), p. 141.

[4] Michael Dobbs, *Down with Big Brother: The Fall of the Soviet Empire* (New York: Alfred A. Knopf, 1997), p. 373.

[5] Boris Yeltsin seems to have shared this view. In his book *The Struggle for Russia* (New York: Random House, 1994, p. 168), Yeltsin declared that he believed more in middle-aged state enterprise managers than in his reform ministers.

[6] This section is largely based on Anders Åslund, *How Russia Became a Market Economy* (Washington, D.C.: Brookings Institution, 1995).

[7] Aleksandr Rutskoi, "Is There a Way out of the Crisis?" *Pravda*, February 8, 1992.

8. G. G. Matiukhin, *Ya byl glavnym bankirom Rossii* (Moscow: Vysshaya shkola, 1993), p. 69. An additional reason for the lack of monetary restraint was that the ruble zone persisted: each country had its own central bank that issued ruble credits independently until the summer of 1993.

9. Diego Gambetta, *The Sicilian Mafia: The Business of Private Protection* (Cambridge, Mass.: Harvard University Press, 1993), p. 1.

10. Reliable data on protection fees are difficult to obtain. These estimates are based on conversations with businessmen and economists in Moscow.

11. Brigitte Granville, "Farewell, Ruble Zone," in Anders Åslund, ed., *Russian Economic Reform at Risk* (London: Pinter, 1995), pp. 65–84. Tajikistan, a marginal economy, continued using Russian rubles.

12. Anders Åslund, Peter Boone, and Simon Johnson, "How to Stabilize: Lessons from Post-Communist Countries," *Brookings Papers on Economic Activity*, vol. 26, no. 1 (1996), pp. 217–313.

13. Anders Åslund, *How Russia Became a Market Economy*, p. 144.

14. A standby agreement is a standard IMF loan program for one year based on a number of conditions concerning primarily budget deficit and monetary expansion.

15. Joseph R. Blasi, Maya Kroumova, and Douglas Kruse, *Kremlin Capitalism: Privatizing the Russian Economy* (Ithaca: Cornell University Press, 1997), p. 193.

16. Ibid., p. 203.

17. See the chapter by Michael McFaul and Nikolai Petrov in this volume.

18. A good example of the arguments used by one leading oilman is the interview with Vagit Alekperov, chief executive officer of Lukoil, "Nuzhno ispol'zovat' opyt Yaponii. . . .", *Kommersant-Daily*, November 11, 1998. Alekperov's suggestions included devaluation, lower taxes for the oil industry (which had already benefited from substantial devaluation), price controls, Central Bank credits for the oil industry, the inflationary emission of money—and continued taxation of the general population.

19. Russian European Center for Economic Policy, *Russian Economic Trends: Monthly Update* (Moscow: Russian European Center for Economic Policy, February 10, 1998), Table 10.

20. Joel S. Hellman, "Winners Take All: The Politics of Partial Reform in Postcommunist Transitions."

21 Andrei Shleifer and Robert Vishny, *The Grabbing Hand: Government Pathologies and Their Cures* (Cambridge, Mass.: Harvard University Press, 1998).

22 Vito Tanzi, "Transition and the Changing Role of Government," paper presented at the IMF conference, "A Decade of Transition: Achievements and Challenges," (Washington, D.C., February 1–3, 1999), Table 5.

23 European Bank for Reconstruction and Development (EBRD), *Transition Report 1995* (London: EBRD, 1995), p. 88.

24 Russian Federation State Tax Service, monthly reports.

25 Vito Tanzi, "Transition and the Changing Role of Government," p. 7.

26 Anders Åslund and Mikhail Dmitriev, eds., *Sotsialnaya politika v period perekhoda k rynku: problemy i resheniya* (Moscow: Carnegie Moscow Center, 1996).

27 Branko Milanovic, *Income, Inequality, and Poverty during the Transition from Planned to Market Economy* (Washington, D.C.: World Bank, 1998), p. 113.

28 See, for example, Martha de Melo, Cevdet Denizer, and Alan Gelb, "From Plan to Market: Patterns of Transition," Policy Research Working Paper 1564 (Washington, D.C.: World Bank, 1996); European Bank for Reconstruction and Development, *Transition Report*; and Bryan T. Johnson and Thomas P. Sheehy, *1996 Index of Economic Freedom* (Washington, D.C.: Heritage Foundation, 1996).

29 Bryan T. Johnson, Kim R. Holmes, and Melanie Kirkpatrick, *1999 Index of Economic Freedom* (Washington, D.C.: Heritage Foundation and the *Wall Street Journal*, 1999), p. 331; James D. Gwartney and Robert A. Lawson, *Economic Freedom of the World: 1997 Annual Report*, as published on the Internet website of the Fraser Institute (www.fraserinstitute.ca), Exhibit 2-2.

30 Transparency International, "The Corruption Perceptions Index," as published on the Internet website of Transparency International (www.transparency.de/documents/cpi/index.html), 1998.

31 A. Blinov, "Maloe predprinimatelstvo i bolshaya politika," *Voprosy ekonomiki*, no. 7 (1996), p. 39.

32 Anders Åslund, "Observations on the Development of Small Private Enterprises in Russia," *Post-Soviet Geography and Economics*, vol. 38, no. 4 (1997), pp. 191–205.

33 Biswajit Banarjee, Vincent Koen, Thomas Krueger, Mark S. Lutz, Michael Marrese, and Tapio O. Saavalainen, *Road Maps of the*

Transition: The Baltics, the Czech Republic, Hungary, and Russia, IMF Occasional Paper no. 127 (Washington, D.C.: International Monetary Fund, 1995).

[34] M. E. Dmitriev, M. Yu. Matovnikov, L. V. Mikhailov, L. I. Sycheva, E. V. Timofeev, and A. Warner, *Rossiiskie banki nakanune finansovoi stabilizatsii* (St. Petersburg: Norma, 1996). In 1997 the Central Bank closed more than 300 Russian banks.

[35] M2 is defined as cash and bank deposits.

[36] Yegor T. Gaidar, "Taktika reform i uroven gosudarstvennoi nagruzki na ekonomiku," *Voprosy ekonomiki,* vol. 70, no. 4 (April 1998), pp. 4–13.

[37] *Russian Economic Barometer,* vol. 7, no. 4, p. 86.

[38] S. Aukutsionek, "Barter v rossiiskoi promyshlennosti," *Voprosy ekonomiki,* vol. 70, no. 2 (February 1998), p. 53.

[39] Ibid., p. 55.

[40] Clifford G. Gaddy and Barry W. Ickes, "Russia's Virtual Economy," *Foreign Affairs,* vol. 77, no. 5 (September/October 1998), pp. 53–67.

[41] Organization for Economic Cooperation and Development, *OECD Economic Surveys: Russian Federation 1997* (Paris: OECD, 1997), p. 181.

[42] Andrei N. Illarionov, "Effektivnost biudzhetnoi politiki v Rossii v 1994–1997 godakh," *Voprosy ekonomiki,* vol. 70, no. 2 (February 1998), p. 24.

[43] Organization for Economic Cooperation and Development, *OECD Economic Surveys: Russian Federation 1997,* p. 181.

[44] Sharon LaFraniere, "A Hotbed of Crime in Cold Siberia: In Gang-Run Coal Land, Authorities Take Cover," *Washington Post,* January 7, 1999, p. A16.

[45] Daniel A. Citrin and Ashkok Kilahiri, eds., "Policy Experiences and Issues in the Baltics, Russia, and Other Countries of the Former Soviet Union," IMF Occasional Paper no. 133 (Washington, D.C.: International Monetary Fund, 1995).

[46] Russia's current VAT rate of 20 percent is comparable to that in other CIS countries and is only slightly higher than the European Union average of 18 percent. A broad Russian consensus favors a sharp reduction. Ironically, the IMF insists on keeping the VAT so high. The profit tax rate of 35 percent was already low by international standards and was lowered to 30 percent in 1999.

The Russian maximum income tax rate of 35 percent is also not high by international standards, although it too should be reduced, since hardly anyone pays at that rate. Reducing the income tax to a flat rate of 20 percent is a common proposal, although the communists advocate higher income taxes for the rich.

At 42 percent, the payroll tax is the highest tax rate and a considerable reduction has been widely demanded. In spite of all the talk of Russian protectionism, import tariffs remain low, averaging about 14 percent. The elimination of offsets and tax exemptions for privileged companies and agriculture are more controversial issues. In any case, tax evasion will inevitably continue to flourish.

47 We take a narrow view of rents as caused through government action, primarily direct or indirect government subsidies. We consider rents as annual flows, not as stocks. We are only concerned with rents going to enterprises, leaving social expenditures aside. Considering the arbitrary tax system and collection practices, a correct tax standard can hardly be established, which makes it impossible to assess the value of tax exemptions appropriately, compelling us to disregard tax exemptions. They have probably diminished slightly over time, because the total tax revenues have fallen and tax exemptions have been strenuously opposed by reformers and the IMF. For the same reason we leave the benefits from barter and offsets aside, which have clearly increased over time. Monopoly rents tend to be estimated at 0.5–1 percent of GDP in a Western economy, and they are likely to be several times larger in Russia, but they are difficult to estimate, which forces us to ignore them. They have probably fallen over time, as regional price differentials have contracted. We also leave aside racketeering fees, which appear to have declined. We are looking at rent seeking from the cost side, while net revenues are much smaller. An official may take a bribe of $10,000 as his private gain, for example, to let somebody seize public assets worth $1 million, which is the public cost. We try to avoid double counting, although we sometimes include the financing of rents and sometimes disbursements.

48 Oil and natural gas prices were on average about one-third of the world market price in 1995, but a free market price would probably have been about two-thirds of the world market price, because

of the high transportation costs. Therefore, the export rent can be assessed at about one-third of exports of oil and natural gas. In 1995 total Russian exports of oil, petroleum products, and natural gas amounted to $39.3 billion, and GDP was $357 billion (Goskomstat Rossii, *Rossiiskii Statisticheskii Yezhegodnik 1997* [Moscow: Goskomstat, 1997], pp. 577, 582, 586; Brunswick Warburg, *Russian Monthly*, Moscow, December 1998, p. 7).

[49] World Bank, *Fiscal Management in Russia: A World Bank Country Study* (Washington D.C.: World Bank, 1996).

[50] Aleksei Lavrov, "Fiscal Federalism and Financial Stabilization," *Problems of Economic Transition*, vol. 5 (May 1996), p. 87.

[51] Daniel Treisman, "Deciphering Russia's Federal Finance: Fiscal Appeasement in 1995 and 1996," *Europe-Asia Studies*, vol. 50, no. 5 (1998), pp. 893–906; Daniel Treisman, "The Politics of Intergovernmental Transfers in Post-Soviet Russia," *British Journal of Political Science*, vol. 26, no. 3 (July 1996), pp. 299–335; Aleksei Lavrov, *Mify i rify Rossiiskogo byudzhetnogo federalizma* (Moscow: Magistr, 1997).

[52] Organization for Economic Cooperation and Development, *OECD Economic Surveys: Russian Federation 1997*, p. 181.

5
Russia and Its
Nearest Neighbors

Sherman W. Garnett and Dmitri Trenin

In its long history, Russia has faced many periods of internal turmoil and reform. Its diplomats have had to cope with periods when internal challenges constrained external ambitions. Russia also has a long and rich history of relations with China, Japan, Turkey, the European powers, and the United States. The historical record allows Russia to measure today's challenges against those of the past. But Russia has no experience of normal state-to-state relations with Ukraine, Belarus, Kazakhstan, or any other of its new neighbors. These countries first appeared in Russian history as contested frontiers and later became part of czarist Russia or the Soviet Union. What history there is stands in the way of Russia seeing these countries as sovereign neighbors.

It is not surprising that Russian foreign-policy makers have yet to come fully to terms with the challenges posed by these new neighbors. For Russian statesmen today, the rise of these countries—particularly the independent countries that make up the Commonwealth of Independent States (CIS)—is easily the greatest of all the discontinuities in the new strategic environment. On the one hand, current Russian policy formally embraces integration on the territory of the USSR as a vital national interest and as the key to the long-term restoration of Russian power in the world beyond. On the other hand, Russia's leaders have not been able to reach agreement with the leaders of most other CIS states on the terms and implementation of this integration. Even those leaders most keen on integration with Russia—such as presidents Aleksandr Lukashenko of Belarus or

Nursultan Nazarbayev of Kazakhstan—have had to confront a Russian policy that is far less sweeping in practice than in its rhetoric.

While some of the new states face serious economic crises, internal or external conflicts, or political instability, most have worked hard to remain sovereign, have pursued at least a modest set of economic and political reforms, and, in the process, have established a broad set of contacts with the world beyond the former USSR. These trends are unlikely to be reversed—even if Russia develops a more effective policy toward its new neighbors than the one currently in place.

Yet, as the August 1998 financial crisis makes plain, such a new and effective Russian policy is not in the offing. The Russian government remains distracted by internal economic problems, political challenges, and the continued weakness of the state. Indeed, Russia's internal problems are likely to exacerbate the trends that worry Moscow most, particularly the ongoing fragmentation of the post-Soviet space, Russia's waning influence there, and the increasing influence of the outside world on what was once an exclusive sphere of Russian interest. Thus, Russian policy toward its newest neighbors must ultimately come to terms with trends that are unfavorable to the kind of integration that President Yeltsin, senior Russian officials, and the foreign policy community as a whole repeatedly embrace as a vital interest of Russia.

This chapter examines the evolution of Russian policy toward these newest neighbors, concentrating specifically on the Commonwealth of Independent States, where Russia has defined an ambitious set of goals but has obtained only modest results. It begins by reviewing the Russian debate over national identity and interest as it applies to the former USSR, then contrasts Russia's ambitious integrationist agenda with its diminished capacity to sustain such a policy. In the second half of the chapter, we examine the new contours of the post-Soviet space, focusing especially on the dilemmas and adjustments of Russian policy toward this increasingly complex and diverse region.

THE NEW STATES AND RUSSIAN IDENTITY

Seven years after the official shedding of communism and the dismantlement of the Soviet Union, Russia is searching for a new sense of its place in the world that points the way beyond current troubles to the restoration of Russian power. Russia's new neighbors play a key role in this search. Among Russia's leadership and foreign policy community, a rough consensus has developed on the need to develop a new identity for the Russian state in the post-Soviet environment. Many in this group subscribe to a traditional geopolitical worldview, sometimes with residual Marxist-Leninist overtones. They see the world primarily as one of states in which territory, population, and natural resources are the principal assets. Interstate struggle—for raw materials and markets, in particular—is at the heart of international relations. Military force remains a useful instrument of policy.

Although some are beginning to draw lessons from the weakness of the Russian state, by and large Russia's foreign policy community remains convinced that Russia must again become a great power— or at least a great regional power. This insistence on the greatness of the Russian state continues to be one of the fundamental elements of the Russian self-image, and it is much stronger among governmental, military, and academic elites than in society at large. For members of this community, Russia's present troubles are regarded as temporary—perhaps only the latest time of troubles in a regular cycle of advance–decline–advance within its long history. In this view, Russia will not remain in chaos for long. After a frank acknowledgment of Russia's current bleak prospects, for example, Andrei Kokoshin, then deputy defense minister, predicted that "in the foreseeable future" Russia could become one of the world's three or four leading nations in terms of socio-economic development and scientific and technological potential.[1] Others, like Yevgeny Primakov, then foreign minister, have stressed the need for Russia to play a leading role in international affairs: "[T]he international situation itself requires that Russia be not merely a historically great power, but a great power right now." Russia's limited capabilities, Primakov argued, should not be seen as a bar to an active world role, because Russian policy is being carried out "by no means on the basis of current circumstances but on the basis of [Russia's] colossal potential."[2]

Since becoming prime minister in September 1998, Primakov has continued to sound the theme of Russia as one of several emerging centers of gravity in a multipolar world, alongside the United States, China, Germany, the European Union, and Japan. All of these centers are competitors within a classical balance-of-power framework, in which no permanent strategic alignments are deemed possible, and mutual deterrence and containment are the principal policy strategies. The Russian foreign policy community rebels against the notion of a unipolar world that endures for a prolonged period. Its members hope that the inherent plurality of the emerging global system will give Moscow an opening to act as a global stabilizer—and thus to regain some of its lost status. Russia should avoid both confrontation and excessive dependency on other powers, they argue, by adopting a posture of equidistance from other power centers, thus guaranteeing Russia's renewed freedom to maneuver.[3]

These hopes are based on several assumptions about the temporary nature of Russia's difficulties and the enduring strengths inherent in Russia itself. Russia's principal asset is its vast natural resources. Russia is also seen as rich in human, especially intellectual, resources, which could help it exploit the wage gap between it and the more developed economies of the West. Other Russians emphasize the country's unique geographical position in the center of Eurasia as a land bridge between Europe and the Asia-Pacific region. This unique geopolitical position ensures that, even if Russia becomes a mere regional power, it will do so in the most important region on earth, adjacent to East and South Asia, the Middle East, and Europe.

Russia's new neighbors, especially those within the Commonwealth of Independent States, play both a psychological and a strategic role in this emerging conception of Russia's restoration as a key center of power. While there are vast differences of opinion over what integration within the former USSR should look like, which states it should include, and by what means it should be realized, few in Moscow's foreign policy community doubt that the first steps toward Russia's reemergence on the world stage must begin in its relations with the new states.[4] Indeed, since 1991, these states have gained the attention in Russian foreign policy originally given to the United States, the West, and what was once called by then foreign minister Andrei Kozyrev and President Boris Yeltsin "the civilized world." At least for some in the Russian leadership and foreign policy community, the turn to the near abroad also represents a turning away from the West itself. The CIS states thus constitute Russia's number-one diplomatic priority—ranking above the West and activating the much talked about eastern or Eurasian dimensions of Russian foreign policy.[5] Even for those who still believe Russian policy must look westward, Russia's new neighbors and the CIS remain a core preoccupation.

Russia's policy goals toward the CIS and the former Soviet space were set forth in a special presidential decree of September 14, 1995, which categorized the CIS as an area of vital interest for Russia—and one to be jealously guarded against trespassers and interlopers. Russia's relations with the states of the CIS are "an important factor for including Russia in world political and economic structures." The presidential decree, combined with numerous high-level statements made before and after it, affirm the priority of Russia's relationship with the states of the CIS, precisely because "all our main vital interests are concentrated on the territory of the CIS." They assert that Russian policy must concern itself with the political, economic, military, and humanitarian stability of these new states, and that it must encourage them to conduct policies that are friendly to Russia. It must strengthen Russia "in the capacity of the leading force for forming a new system of interstate [mezhgosudarstvennye] political and economic relations on the territory of the former USSR." And it must expand integrationist processes in the CIS itself.[6]

At the heart of this policy is a tension between grand ambitions for a Russian-led community and Russia's capabilities to inspire or coerce its neighbors to create such a community. Indeed, the vaunted consensus so many analysts and commentators have seen in Russian foreign policy toward its new neighbors is more an article of faith than a consistent policy. This consensus has often broken down, primarily because of dissent within Russia over the allocation of scarce resources. Of course, there are still those who question existing borders and threaten the use of political, economic, and even military means to restore the union. But most Russians are unwilling to make the sacrifices required to restore a union or even a deeply integrated community. Everyday Russian policy is defined by the struggle between a pragmatic recognition that Russia must make the best of what has come to pass and the hope that the existing trends toward a more fragmented former USSR can be overcome through a combination of "carrot and stick." This leads to a fundamental tension in Russian policy between means and ends.

It is this tension that makes Russia itself one of the key obstacles to normal cooperation and integration on the territory of the former

USSR. It makes Russia reluctant to recognize and build upon the real and more cooperative levers—such as its enormous long-term economic influence, or the cultural and personal ties that remain— to influence the shape of its new neighborhood. It makes Russia suspicious of the sovereignty and independence of its new neighbors or unable to see their new status as anything more than a temporary aberration. Most of all, Russia's overarching ambitions for the restoration of its global importance, large size, and history of being a great power are all at odds with the more modest goals of its new neighbors, who want specific, pragmatic arrangements with Russia that are compatible with their independence and internal stability. This disparity of outlook makes developing a concept of CIS integration a struggle among Russia and the largest and most outward-looking of the new states. It also creates tensions between Russia and the small or troubled states that want not only integration, but also immediate and tangible help from a Russia reluctant or unable to unloose its purse strings.

RUSSIA'S DIMINISHED CAPACITY

A crucial element of Russia's foreign and security policy is its diminished capacity. The essential elements of state power—the basic political structures that make and implement foreign, economic, and military policy—are all in the grip of systemic crisis and transformation. Both the crisis and the reforms aimed at ending this crisis conspire to constrain Russian state power. Ambitious claims to "be not merely a historically great power, but a great power right now" attempt to conceal this weakness from the outside world and perhaps from the Russian leadership itself, but Russia's diminished capacity is a decisive factor in its current policy toward the CIS.[7]

In Russia, basic state institutions have buckled under the enormous strain of change. The state is simply overwhelmed with pressing tasks ranging from providing the legal underpinning for a market economy to restructuring relations between the central government and the regions. Corruption and fragmentation of the old decision-making structures have also taken their toll. As a 1996 draft national security statement complained, "State structures of power are unstable"—a complaint that was still valid in the spring of 1999.[8] It is difficult to see any enduring signs of the central management and implementation of foreign policy. The reason for the state's failure in this area is not President Yeltsin's uncertain health, though his health problems have created long periods of presidential inactivity since 1995, but rather that the old Soviet mechanisms to ensure central control have disappeared, and the work of creating replacement institutions has hardly begun.

Yeltsin and other senior officials regularly lament the "contradictions between the proclaimed course and the actual implementation" of foreign policy.[9] Controversy over Russia's foreign policy direction and implementation arose in the first days of the Federation. Arguments about institutional arrangements and who should lead Russian foreign policy—particularly toward the new neighbors—have been consistent features of the Russian foreign policy debate from 1991 to the present. Since January 1996 Yeltsin has repeatedly reshuffled his national security team. This period has seen three foreign and defense ministers, as well as changes in the cadre and structure of the National Security Council. Yeltsin has formed and re-formed the mechanisms of coordination and oversight for foreign policy several times. Examples include the December 1996 creation of a Foreign Policy Council, the March 1996 decree that returned foreign policy coordination to the Ministry of Foreign Affairs, and the July 1996 creation of a Defense Council (which was abolished in mid-1998). Each change in the foreign policy bureaucracy was accompanied by a promise that the new personnel or bureaucratic structure would end the chaos of making and implementing foreign and security policy, yet that chaos continues.[10]

In fact, chaos at the center has left the ministers and special interest groups within and outside the government free to fill the policy gap. It is by no means true that every minister has his own foreign policy, but many of the most important officials have special prerogatives in their areas of competence. The emerging pattern of action in nuclear technology transfers, arms sales, or military intervention on the periphery reflects the fragmentation of power at the center or the initiatives taken by individual ministers or coalitions of local, ministerial, and industrial representatives without prior coordination within the government. In the former Soviet space, the Russian government has at various times decided to take advantage of these initiatives, to ignore them, or provide them with ex post facto strategic justification—but it does not control them.

Not all problems connected with Russia's policy toward its new neighbors come from the chaos or weakness of the current government. Some are the result of a growing pluralism in Russian political life. The range of interests and actors shaping foreign policy is much wider today than it was during Soviet times. At the moment, these new actors and interests contribute to the chaos of a weak center; in the future, they will continue to shape policy—even after the center has regained its bearings.

The most obvious examples of these new interests and actors are economic ones. Soviet foreign policy had little need to balance security interests with commercial ones, but economic considerations are omnipresent in Russian foreign policy toward its new neighbors. Russia's fiscal constraints and the need to keep the confidence of the International Monetary Fund, the World Bank, and other international lenders continue to constrain the most ambitious integrationist plans. The cost of integrating with an unreformed Belarus has applied a powerful brake on this process. Implementing the various agreements to deepen economic, political, or military cooperation within the former USSR requires a tremendous amount of money. Although the weak economies of Russia's new neighbors are a problem in most respects, in the case of integration that weakness is actually an advantage for them, since the financial burden of implementing any of these agreements now and in the foreseeable future will remain overwhelmingly a Russian one.

The Russian government must now also take into account the interests of Russia's new financial and energy companies. Both Gazprom and Lukoil have taken high profile roles in the development of new oil and gas projects in Kazakhstan and the Caspian Sea. Lukoil joined the consortium to extract Caspian oil even as the Russian government declared itself opposed to separate Azerbaijani moves to develop the oil fields.[11] Official government policy in this area has moved closer to Lukoil's—not the reverse. Gazprom has also moved to negotiate debt for equity swaps with Ukraine. Some analysts have argued that these companies act as instruments of the state, not as independent economic actors, but the evidence suggests that companies like Gazprom and Lukoil are primarily interested in maximizing profits and improving their positions within the emerging markets of the CIS. There are obvious geopolitical benefits to Russia from these activities, but the companies are not creatures of the state. These economic interests act more to modify Russian policy than to advance it.

Russia's regional elites are also becoming foreign policy actors. Regions once deep within the Soviet Union are now part of new and uncertain border zones (for example, the North Caucasus and the *oblasts* bordering Ukraine and Kazakhstan). Ethnic Russian regions of the North Caucasus such as Stavropol and Krasnodar have at times pressured Moscow to suppress what they see as the dangerous separatist aspirations of non-Russian ethnic groups such as the Chechens. Other border regions, in contrast, are beginning to create integrated economic zones. A Russian-Ukrainian border economy has already emerged. One 1996 study by a Ukrainian research institute found that the unregulated informal sector of the economy provided the "main source of income for 2.5 million people, including up to 40 percent of youth in urban and border regions."[12] These figures have almost certainly increased steadily since 1996, although the effects of the 1998 financial crisis will undoubtedly slow their growth, at least in the short run. The Russian-Ukrainian border regions and communities along the periphery of Russia are creating economic, political, and social ties quite apart from formal state ties. Regions rich in natural resources or dominated by declining military production are also active in cross-border commerce. Producers of diamonds, gold, timber, and jet fighters and other military technology are unwilling to let the center control what they see as their resources. They are increasingly presenting the center with faits accomplis as they make deals of their own with foreign companies and governments. The economic power of regions rich in resources and situated along key trading routes will continue to make itself felt in Russian policy toward its new neighbors.

Russia also faces severe economic constraints in pursuing its foreign policy aims. The resources Russia can devote to any foreign or security policy problem have shrunk dramatically: Russian GDP is today perhaps one-fourth of what the Soviet Union's GDP was in the late 1980s—and it is still declining. Russia has experienced negative economic growth for a decade. It now spends a much smaller percentage of its state budget on national security and foreign policy than did the Soviet Union, and defense and foreign spending must compete with other demands on the budget ranging from unpaid salaries to basic social services.

The privatization process is of greater long-term importance than the current economic decline, since it has removed vast resources from the direct control of the state. The state can no longer manage most enterprises directly, except where a sitting government official and outside partners have become the actual or de facto owners of a firm. The state must now tax wealth that lies in private hands. But while some private resources have been mobilized for state ends, most notably the private donations that helped sustain Russian forces in Chechnya, most of those now in control of newly privatized assets have shown little zeal to use their newfound wealth and power for the good of the state.

Russia's natural resources, size, and long-term economic prospects still constitute real levers over the policies of its neighbors, particularly those most dependent on Russia for energy and other basic commodities. But the management of these resources is no longer simply in the government's hands. Russia's energy companies and banks may pursue policies that place them in privileged positions or that even disrupt the economies of the new states, but it can no longer be presumed that these companies are acting for the government or out of any sense of Russian state interest.

Finally, a key instrument of Russian policy toward the new neighbors is the military, which is in precipitous decline even as it expands its involvement and commitments throughout the former USSR. The military's dramatic failure in Chechnya and its inability to be an effective lever for the resolution of ongoing disputes elsewhere (such as in Tajikistan, Georgia, or Moldova) are obvious signs of military overstretch. Furthermore, this level of military involvement in the new borderlands consumes resources that the military desperately needs for reform.

The level of decline in the military is staggering. In 1988 the Soviet Union had more than 5 million men under arms, more than 200 heavy divisions, 50,000 main battle tanks, and 8,000 aircraft. This military was deployed far forward in Eastern Europe. In 1998 the Russian armed forces had fewer than 1.2 million people, although a substantial number of additional forces remain outside the control of the Ministry of Defense (namely, in the Ministry of Internal Affairs, the Border Guards, and other paramilitary structures). Almost half of those in the armed forces are officers. In the Russian armed forces proper, there are approximately 80 divisions, slightly more than

15,500 main battle tanks, and 2,000–3,000 combat aircraft. Moreover, Western sources estimate that only 30 of Russia's ground divisions (and 12 of 26 brigades) are even minimally operational. Sources in Moscow in mid-1996 put the number of operational divisions at no more than eight.[13] Despite subsequent efforts at military reform, the number of operational units has, if anything, declined. Similar problems affect the readiness of the air, air defense, and especially the naval forces. Russian nuclear forces are better off, since they occupy the highest priority in the defense budget. Even so, only a modest portion of the total force of 8,000–10,000 warheads is operationally ready.

Budget limitations also contribute to the underfunding of military research and development, the failure to procure new equipment or to provide basic support for officers, enlisted men, and their families, and the lack of adequate field training and other crucial building blocks of an effective military. In October 1996 Igor Rodionov, then defense minister, warned that, "because of the chronic shortage of funds, Russia's armed forces reached the limit beyond which extremely undesirable and even uncontrollable processes may arise."[14] In February 1996 Yeltsin bluntly stated that "military reform made virtually no headway in Russia last year."[15] Yeltsin replaced Rodionov in May 1997 with Igor Sergeyev, commander of the Strategic Rocket Forces. With Sergeyev came a renewed commitment to military reform and an increasing anxiety about what could happen to the armed forces if reform is not carried out. Yeltsin paid more attention to the matter in the latter half of 1997, but no real sustained progress has been made since then. Some structural changes in the commands have been carried out, but the core problems remain unpaid wages, low morale, poor housing and material support for officers, and a lack of training.

These problems give rise to serious differences of opinion both inside and outside the military on the proper course of reform. Part of the reason for the failure to reform is external, particularly the political chaos and the economic constraints outlined above; part of it is internal, for the military has so far refused to make necessary choices. It became mired in Chechnya, Tajikistan, and elsewhere around the former USSR. It is forced to fund its nuclear capabilities, which it considers essential to the retention of Russia's global standing. And it seeks new bases and military-to-military arrangements with its new neighbors—arrangements in which it is asked or seeks to play the role of protector and benefactor. The Russian military continues to be stretched extremely thinly, with no limit in sight to the demands upon its meager resources.

The combination of these factors—political confusion, economic constraints, and a military in crisis—serves to limit Russian power, even within its own so-called neighborhood. Although Russia's size and resources (both present and future) dwarf those of its neighbors, those neighbors present collective challenges that exceed Russia's current capabilities. Russian policy thus may aim for a coordinated approach to the whole of the CIS, but Russian capabilities ensure that Russia will have to make choices, establish priorities, and settle for something much less than its leaders currently would like.

RUSSIA'S DIVERSE NEIGHBORHOOD

Russia's policy has an additional obstacle: the new neighbors themselves are much more diverse, their sovereignty is more deeply rooted, and their links to the world beyond the former USSR are growing faster than Russian leaders expected. Some weak and potentially unstable states like Belarus and Tajikistan continue to look to Russia for fiscal and political support. Ukraine, Kazakhstan, and Uzbekistan, however, are steadily solidifying their links to the outside world. Moreover, all of the CIS countries, including Russia, are redirecting substantial portions of their trade outside the CIS. The ex-Soviet economic, political, and military infrastructure is crumbling. The ethnic Russian and Russian-speaking diaspora—often placed at the center of debate about integration and Russia's interest in the former USSR—is wary of being seen as disloyal to its adopted countries; there are few signs that it could be mobilized as an instrument of Russian foreign policy. And even where there is nostalgia for the old system, there are few inside or outside Russia who believe it can be restored.

Given Russia's diminished capabilities and the need to focus on its own internal problems, it is unlikely that this trend toward increasing diversification can be arrested. Russia's neighbors outside the CIS are moving away from their old links to the imperial and Soviet space even faster than the CIS countries are. Nearly all of the Baltic states and the former non-Soviet Warsaw Pact nations look west for their future prosperity and security ties. Poland, Hungary, and the Czech Republic became formal members of the North Atlantic Treaty Organization (NATO) in the spring of 1999. Turkey and Iran, though they have taken different stances with regard to the changes in the former USSR, have both become more active players in the Caucasus and Central Asia. To Russia's east, China appears on the road to great-power status early in the next century.

In the next five or ten years, the notion of a single geographical entity known as the former Soviet Union is likely to disappear from popular usage altogether, except among historians. It will be replaced by new designations focusing on geographic, cultural, and economic differences. One basic distinction will increasingly be between Islamic and European states. Another will be between the energy-rich and the energy-poor states. A group of energy-producing states—including Kazakhstan, Turkmenistan, and Azerbaijan—has already emerged, although the political and economic wrangling among them, Russia, and other interested powers is by no means completed. Moreover, estimates of the potential oil and gas reserves have often been exaggerated, while low world energy prices and the high costs of constructing pipelines put additional dampers on the emergence of these states. A third distinction will be geographic. The group of states in the European space, for example, has been and will continue to be profoundly influenced by such developments as the enlargement of NATO, the expansion of the European Union, and, most recently, the NATO intervention in Kosovo. Each of these emerging groups has new geopolitical challenges and options, as new and resurrected notions of a Black Sea, South Asian, or inner Asian region now cut across the boundaries of the former Soviet Union and connect portions of this territory with the outside world.

Unfortunately, it is also likely that differentiation within the former USSR will continue on the basis of internal stability, economic progress, and external threats. Tajikistan remains a divided state with a weak central government. Despite a December 1996 agreement between its government and the united opposition that was brokered jointly by Moscow and Tehran, there is still a great danger that Tajikistan will come to resemble Afghanistan in the near future. The fighting has halted in Abkhazia, Nagorno-Karabakh, and the Transdniester, although no working settlement is in place to ensure that the current cease-fires become permanent settlements. The main threats in these regions do not come from strong military forces, either within the regions or outside them, but from a fragmented and chaotic security environment.

In this more differentiated region, there will still be states with strong ties to Russia—by necessity and by choice. Weak and unstable states whose leaderships are threatened by internal problems will cling to Moscow for support. Internally strong states, such as Armenia, will also look to Moscow out of self interest. Historical preoccupations with other old and new neighbors explain why still other states will continue to look to Moscow.

Yet this view of the post-Soviet space suggests a challenge for Russia that is at odds with the one the Russian leadership has so publicly proclaimed for itself. The challenge will not be to create a unified and highly integrated commonwealth, but to manage the increasing differentiation of the former Soviet space—creating both strong and integrated ties where this is possible but also forging stable state-to-state bonds where integration is not feasible.

Moscow has made the first steps in this direction. Since 1995 Russian policy makers have come to recognize that progress on integration is unlikely to come through giant steps taken by the CIS as a whole, but rather through smaller steps made by individual CIS member states or groups of them. Russia clearly differentiates the CIS states based on their relative economic and geopolitical importance and their willingness to integrate, but it has not abandoned the goal of a more general integration for the former Soviet Union. Yet a survey of the key emerging regions of the former USSR—the states of the former western USSR and the Caucasus and Central Asia—reveals precisely the futility of wholesale integration, although by no means the end of Russian influence or interests.

THE NEW EASTERN EUROPE: BELARUS, UKRAINE, AND MOLDOVA

The shape of the new Eastern Europe is crucial for Russia. Belarus and Ukraine belonged to the czarist and Soviet empires, while the territories of Moldova have long figured prominently in Moscow's drive toward southeastern Europe. Russians see Belarus, Ukraine, and northern Kazakhstan as united to Russia by strong historical, linguistic, cultural, and even religious bonds. More than half of all ethnic Russians from the former USSR who live outside the Russian Federation are in Belarus and Ukraine, where they make up one-fifth and one-tenth of the populations, respectively. These 13 million people are fully integrated in their new countries and do not think of themselves as foreigners in them. Moscow sees these states, along with Kazakhstan, as natural partners for political, economic, and security integration.

Russian policy has focused on tying Belarus and Ukraine to Moscow. A Russian-dominated Slavic Union, though not endorsed officially, remains a popular conception among Russia's leading politicians and foreign policy experts. Although the leaders of the three Slavic nations agreed in December 1991 on forming a commonwealth that many observers inside and outside the former USSR feared was the first step toward such a union, the subsequent histories of Belarus and Ukraine could not be more different with respect to Russian hopes for integration. Belarus has pursued closer ties with Russia, culminating in a bilateral agreement on substantial integration in March 1996 and a treaty creating a Russian-Belarus Commonwealth in April 1997. Ukraine has just as doggedly resisted any bilateral or multilateral arrangement that would constrain its sovereignty. Russian policy has consistently underestimated the staying power of Ukraine as a state, assuming that ethnic divisions, economic collapse, or the simple inexperience of its leaders would lead to the demise of the Ukrainian state. Russia has also underestimated the burden it would bear if it had to bail out either of these states. The financial costs of integration have continually constrained Russian implementation of a broad set of bilateral agreements with Belarus, including the 1996 and 1997 agreements mentioned above. The constitutional crisis in Belarus, which came to a head in November 1996, also demonstrated both Russia's continued interest in the stability of its neighbor and its limited influence over the key players in Belarusian politics. The compromise mediated by then prime minister Chernomyrdin between the Belarusian president and the opposition quickly fell apart, as Lukashenko pressed ahead with a new constitution that gave him increased authority. Ambitious plans for some form of union of the two states broke down in early 1997, and even the more modest agreement they then concluded revealed doubts and concerns about integration in both countries.

Belarus

Because of its geopolitical position between Russia and Central Europe, Belarus is of vital importance to Moscow. The Belarusian leadership, intelligentsia, and population at large have been slow to accept their newfound independence or to embrace the political and economic reforms needed to break decisively with the past. In fact, President Lukashenko's agenda for the country rests primarily not on sound political and economic policies but on the patience of the Belarusian people and Russian help.

Nonetheless, relations between Russia and Belarus, unburdened by any major historical problems, could be a model of voluntary integration within the CIS. The primary hurdles to that integration are Moscow's inability to integrate Belarus within its financial and economic system and Minsk's rigid economic system and domestic political problems. The potential costs of integration have become so controversial in Russia, particularly among those charged with managing the economy, that Lukashenko felt compelled to dismiss "the prejudice that Belarus is allegedly sponging on Russia and wants to live at Russia's expense" in a speech to the Russian Duma in November 1996.[16] As long as Belarus remains mired in political authoritarianism and economic planning, however, it will remain a burden for Russia and the "odd man out" in a region largely defined by success in implementing (or at least by the serious attempt to implement) political and economic reforms.

Belarus also offers a convenient transit corridor that extends to Central and Western Europe, and almost to Kaliningrad. Through close ties to Russia, Belarus gains a friend to sustain it through difficult times. But the November 1996 political crisis revealed just how much is still undecided. Lukashenko's moves toward integration with Russia and his one-man rule at home sparked a small but determined opposition. On the Russian side, the debates in 1996 and 1997 put the issue of what integration will cost squarely before the Russian leadership and people. There is little doubt that Russia is prepared to send senior political figures, like former prime minister Chernomyrdin, to help mediate political crises in Minsk. It is less certain that Russia will indefinitely provide the economic support that Lukashenko's policies require. In fact, the coming of Russia's own economic crisis in August 1998 threatened existing support for Belarus and made its expansion to cover full-scale economic integration quite impossible.

Ukraine

Ukraine is probably Russia's most important neighbor. Unfortunately, the early resentment and suspicion with which Moscow greeted Ukrainian independence has not been fully superseded by normalized, state-to-state relations. But in general the bilateral relationship has demonstrated a greater degree of pragmatism than many in the outside world expected. Perennial crises over dual citizenship, borders, energy debts, or the division and basing of the Black Sea fleet routinely flare up and are put out by senior-level officials—but their crisis resolutions often unravel after the first round of expert meetings. In 1997 the two countries took an important step beyond this pattern by concluding formal agreements on bilateral relations and the division and basing of the Black Sea fleets. These agreements, however, still require the support of both sides to ensure their successful implementation; at the moment neither country has the fiscal or political resources to give these issues the attention they require.

In addition, serious impediments to the further development of normal relations exist in both countries. Within Ukraine, some political forces consider comprehensive agreements with Russia a clear threat to Ukrainian sovereignty. The most pro-active, pro-Russian elements in Ukraine seek economic ties with Russian financial and industrial groups that will clearly benefit not just themselves but the country as a whole. A bigger problem by far lies in Moscow. Many Russian foreign policy analysts see the current distance between the two countries as unnatural and temporary. Ukraine's obvious success in stabilizing its statehood at first angered, then surprised, and now merely annoys many in the Russian government and foreign policy community. Despite the May 1997 Russian-Ukrainian agreement, the status of the Crimean Peninsula or the city of Sevastopol as Ukrainian territory remains a sore spot for some in Russia and a staple of political posturing among its opposition and high-level governmental figures alike. Ironically, it is precisely the periodic campaigns for a "Russian Sevastopol"—a theme now incorporated in Moscow Mayor Yuri Luzhkov's presidential campaign—

that help consolidate the Ukrainian political elite and confirm its suspicions about Russia's long-term intentions.

Because Ukrainian independence is, above all else, independence from Moscow, any new political association between the two will be slow in coming. If it does come, it is not likely to come on terms many Russian politicians now desire, namely, a resubordination of Ukraine or at least a far-reaching alteration of the terms of Ukrainian sovereignty. In the near term, Russia has placed its emphasis on keeping Ukraine within the CIS and on expanding economic ties between the two states. Russia and Ukraine remain important trading partners, but they and other CIS countries have also increased trade with the outside world. Despite increased Russian tariffs on key Ukrainian exports in 1996–1997 and the economic difficulties both countries have experienced since 1998, Russia remains Ukraine's most important export market. Russia supplies 90 percent of Ukraine's oil and 80 percent of its natural gas. The Ukrainian debt to Russia is approximately $6 billion. Ukrainian migrant workers, ubiquitous in Russia, are an important source of support for their relatives in Ukraine.[17]

The prime vehicles of greater integration are neither CIS economic institutions such as the Customs Union (which Ukraine refuses to join) nor the largely symbolic Interstate Economic Committee, but Russian or Russian-Ukrainian financial and industrial groups and banks. There are also many on both sides of the border who want to preserve and expand natural economic and cultural links. Ukraine is an obvious market and an investment target for these firms and various regional groupings.

Fortunately, contentious political issues between Russia and Ukraine have not led to a genuine crisis. The Russian government has firmly resisted nationalist pressure to lay claim to Crimea or the city of Sevastopol or to cut oil and gas supplies. The issue of former Soviet nuclear weapons in Ukraine was satisfactorily resolved in a trilateral arrangement with the United States; by mid-1996 the denuclearization of Ukraine was complete. Despite strongly worded declarations denouncing one another's approaches, the two sides found a solution to the division of the Black Sea fleet and the long-term basing of its Russian component in Crimea. Neither country has shown that it has the financial resources to sustain the fleet under current conditions. Pragmatists in both governments have found ways to manage their respective interests while avoiding confrontation. To date, they—not the ideologues—have controlled the relationship.

Moldova

Moldova is of much less importance to Russia's long-term interest, yet Russia has been active in that country due to the presence of the former Soviet Fourteenth Army and the situation in the breakaway Transdniestrian Republic, both of which have given Russia a cause and an excuse for intervention in Moldovan affairs. Russia is committed to helping Moldova achieve a settlement of the long-simmering conflict over Transdniester, although it is also the de facto protector of the Russian-speaking Transdniestrians, and it keeps a military force (now less than 2,500 men) in the country. Under the weight of the conflict with the Transdniestrians as well as of the Russian intervention to suppress it, Moldova joined the CIS, ensuring that it will not drift too far from Russia's grasp in the near term. Another compelling reason for joining was to regain access to former Soviet markets. Yet Moldova's export potential to Russia, like that of its CIS neighbors, has been hard hit by Russia's economic crisis. Moldova's still underdeveloped and sometimes contentious relationship with Romania deprives it of an obvious partner and counterbalance to Russian influence.

Moscow has long seen the Balkans and Southeastern Europe as an area of its interest. A strong Russian influence in Moldova, it is believed, improves Russia's position with respect to the Balkan peninsula—and helps to keep Moldova focused on the former USSR and not on its potential links to Romania or Europe as a whole.

One wild card in Moldovan-Russian relations is the former Fourteenth Army. Although it has been greatly reduced in size, its deployment in the Transdniester region and its strong ties to the local separatists there remain knotty problems. A Russian-Moldovan agreement to withdraw this army remains in effect, but both sides have concerns about whether the withdrawal would take place in an orderly manner. The Moldovans in particular fear that the equipment of the withdrawing units would find its way to Transdniestrian fighters. The potential instability of both the status quo and the withdrawal of Russian forces brought new momentum to the talks and a new interlocutor to the table in 1997, when Ukraine joined Russia as a coguarantor of the mediation process. President Kuchma has also stated that Ukraine would be willing to provide peacekeeping forces to work with Russian forces already in the region. The differences between the Transdniestrians and the Moldovan central government remain substantial: Transdniestrian demands for de facto sovereignty and membership in the CIS in late 1997 provided a stark reminder that although the military conflict has been frozen, no political resolution is imminent.

THE SOUTHERN BELT: THE CAUCASUS AND CENTRAL ASIA

Russia's approach to the southern belt of CIS states is based on the existence of several serious conflicts, vast energy and other resources, and the perceived high degree of instability in the area. The weakest of these states—including Tajikistan, Kyrgyzstan, and Georgia—have turned to Russia for direct support (in the case of Georgia, under considerable duress). Both Armenia and Kazakhstan believe that they require close ties with Russia to withstand actual or potential local threats to their survival—even as they remain cognizant of potential threats from Russia itself. Turkmenistan has carved out its own special relationship with Russia, although it often joins the most independent-minded CIS states in their defiance of Russian initiatives. And the southern belt also includes Uzbekistan and Azerbaijan, two states with ambitions to break free from the old relationship with Moscow and to become influential regional actors in their own right.

Russian forces are deeply involved in conflicts ranging from Abkhazia to South Ossetia and Tajikistan. It is in this region that Russia's Chechen debacle is most closely analyzed, both for its immediate effect on adjacent regions and for what it says about Russian power. Russia's defeat by Chechen fighters will undoubtedly have far-reaching consequences for the calculations of the leaders of the Caucasian and Central Asian states, as well as of their neighbors.

Despite Russia's apparently formidable military advantages over the vastly weaker or nonexistent military forces of the states of the Caucasus and Central Asia, the military dimension may turn out to be Russia's least effective lever of influence, particularly if indigenous forces decide to challenge rather than to acquiesce to this military power. The utility of brute force is limited even in what the Russians regard as an unstable south. Waging a war against determined guerrilla fighters supported by the bulk of the local population is very costly; winning such a war is extremely difficult. The Russian people and military have already experienced one Chechnya and are unlikely to seek out another. The key measures of military influence are no longer simply the ratio of tanks, planes, and artillery—where Russia is likely to remain the strongest power by far—but rather the geographic terrain, the attitudes of the local population, and the capacity of the Russian people and political elite to understand and support the application of military power in what are increasingly alien and far-off places.

If this lesson of the Chechnya war becomes part of the Moscow consensus—and there are signs that a large number of the Russian foreign policy establishment view the Chechnya experience in this way—it could effect a profound change in Russia's attitude toward this southern belt of states. In addition to traditional security concerns, Russia is also coming to understand the economic challenges and opportunities in these states, especially in Kazakhstan and in the Caspian Sea area. The development of Caspian and Central Asian energy resources has sparked an international competition that Russian companies—and increasingly the Russian government—have entered.

Thus even in the south, Russia cannot rest content with the old tactics of exploiting political weaknesses and divisions within the new states. In Georgia, Russia tried these tactics by first tilting toward the Abkhazian separatists and then obtaining a set of concessions from the leaders in Tbilisi that brought Georgia into the CIS and offered Russia military bases and equipment in that country. Yet these concessions were themselves predicated on deeper Russian involvement in resolving the Georgia-Abkhazia conflict, particularly in returning ethnic Georgian refugees to Abkhazia. To date, Russia has been unable to carry out this part of the bargain, leading Georgian President Eduard Shevardnadze and a large majority in the Georgian parliament to question the validity of the military accords with Moscow. At the same time, the Russian State Duma has yet to ratify major elements of the Russia-Georgia relationship, suggesting—as with other integrationist policies in Belarus and elsewhere—that the Russian leadership's stated intentions far outstrip its ability to follow through. Indeed, the lesson of Abkhazia may well be that, for the foreseeable future, Russia has the power to keep existing conflicts in the CIS frozen but not to resolve them.

In Kazakhstan, the Caspian basin, and elsewhere, Russian economic interests have used their size, historical ties, and transportation links to insert themselves into energy and other economic deals. Russian capital could become a more effective means of projecting Russian influence than military power. But Russia's current economic problems and the cutthroat competition between these interests certainly slow down progress toward a wholesale transformation of Russian thinking on economic levers of influence. Moscow has won from Almaty a large share of the Caspian Pipeline Project; Russian oil companies are actively involved in Azerbaijan; Russian business interests are considering investing in oil transit through Georgia; Russia's Gazprom is taking over Turkmenistan's gas exports. In a stunning postwar move, Russia is even planning to transit oil through Chechnya. The prospect of transporting some 60 million tons of oil, much of it through Russian territory, is a primary influence on Russia's policy in the Caspian Sea basin. If these policies do indeed represent something more than a change of tactics, they would signify an important shift away from the old geopolitical conceptions of power toward a positive-sum view of competition and interests that is characteristic of Europe, North America, and the rest of the Western world.

Yet geopolitical dimensions are by no means absent from Russian policy in the Caucasus and Central Asia. Georgia and Armenia are regarded as potential political allies, but relations with each country are burdened by unresolved internal and interstate conflicts that Russia can neither resolve nor fully suppress. In Central Asia, Kazakhstan and Kyrgyzstan form an important crossroads between Russia, China, and the Moslem world that Russia does not want to surrender. The large numbers of Russians and Russian-speakers who settled in the northern and western parts of Kazakhstan create additional linkages. Geopolitical arguments underpin the Russian commitment to defend Tajikistan's border, where Russia has been trying since 1992 to prevent the country from fragmenting. At present, the local government is fully dependent on Russia and ostensibly loyal to it—but not fully in control of the country. The constant pressure from the domestic and émigré opposition, as well as the danger of a spillover from the continuing war in Afghanistan—of special concern after the fall of Kabul to the Taliban in September 1996—work to undermine Russia's long-term position there. Conscious of this predicament, Russia has intensified efforts to cooperate with Iran in brokering a peace settlement between the Tajik factions.

The Tajik civil war has also strained Russia's relations with Uzbekistan, an aspiring regional power in Central Asia. Seeing Moscow as weak and distant, Tashkent has refused the role of Russia's regional lieutenant and has diversified its foreign policy and economic links to the outside world. It has even gone so far as to challenge Moscow's hitherto unquestioned domination of CIS military structures. Tashkent aims to make itself in some respects the Central Asian equivalent of Ukraine. Other Central Asian states are bypassing Russia and establishing direct transportation and communication links with both immediate and distant neighbors. The ancient Silk Road from China and Central Asia to Iran, Turkey, and Europe is being revived in the form of a rail link. Other projects now being planned will connect Central Asia to the Persian Gulf and South Asia. Though these projects remain modest and will take years to develop fully, the trend lines are clear.

THE ROLE OF THE OUTSIDE WORLD

The Russian leadership and foreign policy community regard the CIS countries as lying clearly within the Russian sphere of interest, if not sphere of influence. The activities of the outside world on the territory of the former USSR are perceived as at best an intrusion and at worst a serious threat to Russia's national interests. There are of course anti-Russian forces at work in some of the ongoing conflicts, but for the most part the outside world has gotten involved on the territory of the former Soviet Union not to constrain or replace Russia, but because the breakdown of the old Soviet frontiers has resulted in new political, diplomatic, economic, and even military ties.

New and developing transportation links will erode Moscow's role as the single hub of the former USSR. Whatever the short-term outcomes of the struggle over pipelines, in the long run there are certain to be alternative routes that bypass the existing Russian-dominated system. Iran is unlikely to remain a pariah state forever.

China has shown interest in developing energy links with both Russia and Central Asian states. In at least parts of the former USSR, economic development in the next decade will create a new transportation and communication infrastructure to supplement the existing one.

For a time it seemed that NATO enlargement eastward had become the most important crisis in postcommunist Russia's relations with the West. From the Russian perspective, NATO enlargement is but another example of encroachment from the outside world. And although the new members admitted in the first wave of enlargement (Poland, Hungary, and the Czech Republic) do not include countries of the former USSR, three such countries—Estonia, Latvia, and Lithuania—have announced their desire to join NATO in the future. Perhaps more important, the extension of NATO's boundary eastward will increase Western interest in the stability of the states that will now be on NATO's new border, including the Baltic states, Belarus, and Ukraine. NATO will have to take a greater interest in these states precisely because their internal and external policies will have such an important effect on Poland—and thus on the Alliance as a whole.

While Poland's membership in NATO is highly undesirable for the Russians, a second wave enlargement involving the Baltic states is completely unacceptable. Increased Russian efforts to pressure the Baltic states to forego NATO membership—and heightened Baltic concerns that such pressures cannot be resisted except by joining the Alliance—could create a destabilizing situation along the new fault line. Fortunately, Russia has tried to balance its insistence on Baltic neutrality with progress in defining state borders and reducing the concentration of its military forces in the region. In late 1997 President Yeltsin and senior Russian officials proposed new security initiatives for the Baltic states and the Baltic Sea region; these focused on additional conventional and nuclear weapons reductions and possible confidence-building measures. Several of these proposals, however, were explicitly linked to the Baltic states renouncing interest in NATO membership—demonstrating that even positive trends in Russian-Baltic relations can still be hijacked by Russia's opposition to a new round of NATO enlargement. Although the Baltic problem may be the most imminent, NATO enlargement will shape Russian policy toward all of its new neighbors. Ukraine, for example, will become a de facto buffer zone between Russia and NATO. Kiev will have to perform a complicated balancing act or face serious domestic and international problems. The integration of Belarus and Russia could stimulate a quicker unification of the defense policies of Minsk and Moscow, but Russia's financial crisis and unresolved problems for both governments make this faster track unlikely. It is worth noting, however, that although NATO enlargement has absorbed the bulk of Russian attention, a parallel set of problems will likely emerge from the enlargement of the European Union to the edge of the former USSR and—in the case of Estonia—into the former USSR itself.

Moscow has also tried to use NATO enlargement as a reason to consolidate the 1995 Tashkent Treaty on Collective Security as an effective security alliance. This treaty joins Armenia, Belarus, Kazakhstan, Kyrgyzstan, Russia, and Tajikistan in a loose alliance. As might be expected, the basic military capabilities of this alliance are weak. More important, however, the differentiation in security perceptions among its members makes many of them indifferent to the supposed threat of NATO enlargement. Russia's calls to create an alliance to counter NATO are more likely to complicate the search for a CIS security mechanism than to have a consolidating effect. The greatest danger is that the current low levels of military forces in Central and Eastern Europe could be forsaken due to military moves and countermoves surrounding NATO enlargement and Russian response. While many options for counter-measures hinted at by Russian officials are unrealistic, there could be consequences for both conventional and nuclear arms control. Whether Russia actually deploys tactical nuclear systems or not, enlargement will undoubtedly make more acceptable the current minority view that there is a need to rethink policy regarding these weapons.

At the other end of Eurasia, China is emerging as a power of real significance. There has been much less debate about China's potential for shaping the post-Soviet region than about NATO's, but in many respects, China's capacity to do so is the greater of the two. China is already making its economic influence felt throughout Central Asia and the Russian Far East. Demographically, China dwarfs the small populations of Russians and various Central Asian nationalities on the other side of the old Sino-Soviet border.

In Central Asia, Russia and China are essentially separated by smaller and weaker Muslim states. The two big powers and three

Central Asian border states have signed multilateral and bilateral agreements to demilitarize their borders and to cooperate in the fight against instability and ethnic separatism. But while China will police its own territory and let Russia handle security problems on the CIS side of the border, China has already become active economically and politically in Kazakhstan and Kyrgyzstan. Russia has tried to head off future problems by fashioning a broad-based strategic partnership with Beijing: the two sides have largely resolved serious border issues, undertaken new measures to increase military transparency, and expanded bilateral trade. Russia has also attempted to upgrade relations with Tokyo to balance its ties with Beijing.[18]

At this point, the primary impediments to Russian influence in the former USSR are not other large states, but instability and armed conflicts within and just outside the CIS, such as the ongoing wars in Tajikistan and Afghanistan. Russia appears just strong enough to contain these conflicts—but not strong enough to resolve or suppress them. On the surface, these conflicts seem to confirm the need for continued Russian presence in the region, but as long as that presence is inadequate to the challenges at hand, these conflicts have the potential to erode Russia's power and influence there.

In the longer term, the region as a whole will forge new links to the outside world. In the next five years and beyond, these links alone will not erode Moscow's position, but eventually they will create economic, political, and even security alternatives to the current Moscow-led Tashkent Security Alliance. Over time, Russia will become an increasingly alien presence in the pervading Islamic culture. And Russia is unlikely to be as economically dynamic as China. These trends, together with new communications lines, railroads, and pipelines, will give the states of the region other options. The rise of Uzbekistan to the status of a regional power will also complicate Russia's current political, military, and security arrangements. All of these trends are at work, even if they are slow to develop their full potential to alter the current status quo.

Turkey, Iran, and other Islamic states have also increasingly become actors in their own right in portions of the former USSR. Turkish or Iranian inroads have not led to the recreation of serious diplomatic and military friction—the new great game foretold by

some analysts. In fact, Russia and Iran have largely reversed historical patterns of competition by coming to share the view that instability in the Caucasus is a common threat. Russia's attitude toward
Turkey is schizophrenic: a virtual explosion of trade and human
contacts has been accompanied by the revival of historical suspicions. The present conflict of interest with regard to pipeline routes,
the political orientation of Azerbaijan, and the general situation in
the Northern Caucasus are all perceived in terms of nineteenth-
century geopolitics.[19]

Iran, Turkey, Pakistan, and other Islamic states are also bearers
of Islamic culture. On that level, they have much more in common
with the states of Central Asia, Azerbaijan, and even enclaves within
the Russian Federation than does Russia itself. The process of re-
Islamization has begun throughout the Muslim parts of the former
Soviet Union. What Russia fears (and almost certainly exaggerates)
is that this process will bring Islamic extremism and instability. The
wars the Russians have been waging in the last decade and a half
have been with Moslem forces: Afghanistan (1979–1989), Tajikistan
(1992–), and Chechnya (1994–1996). While there is no reason why
these conflicts must be seen as "clashes of civilizations," many Russian participants do see them as such. For some, Islamic extremism
is a clear and present danger: the unstable states of Afghanistan and
Tajikistan are especially vulnerable to extremist Islamic influences,
while the still weak state structures of many of the Islamic states of
the former USSR make them potentially vulnerable as well.

What is striking about these and other outside influences that are
just beginning to be felt is that they signify a dramatic reversal of
the historical flow of power in Eurasia. For the first time in decades,
political, economic, and even military power is flowing from the
outside into the heart of Eurasia. What happens on the outer rim—
in China, India, Pakistan, Iran, and Turkey—has an increasing
impact at the center of the Eurasian landmass. The Soviet state
effectively sealed itself off from the outside world. It attempted to
influence the rimlands, not always successfully, but it was rarely
influenced by them. This change of the old patterns is of momentous
significance in Eurasia and is likely to be a source of continuing
shock to Russia. The shock is more likely than not to come on the
territory of one of Russia's new neighbors—precisely because these
countries are still not seen by most Russian policy makers as fully

independent states with interests and ambitions of their own. Russia expects to have German, Chinese, American, or Japanese challenges; it does not expect challenges from Ukraine.

The outside world's gains do not leave Russia powerless, nor do they necessarily come at Russia's expense. Over the next several years, Russia will continue to enjoy tremendous advantages as a large and more powerful neighbor, as the owner of important energy and communications infrastructure, and as a power that will unquestionably show an interest in the political, economic, and security concerns of its neighbors. It needs to understand how to transform these advantages into a sustainable strategy.

What Russia cannot do is to halt the trends that will make it relatively less influential in these states and that will make the various states of the outside world relatively more influential. Russia does not have the material, cultural, or political power to compel the re-formation of a new union or to entice these new states into one. It will have to pursue a strategy that reaches well beyond its near abroad. Russia's policy in Central Asia must come to see China, Iran, Pakistan, India, and Turkey not simply as powers to be fended off, but as active partners and peaceful competitors. Likewise, Russia's policy toward the former western USSR must facilitate the development of productive relations with NATO, especially with its newest member states of Central Europe.

In the mid-1990s, Russian analysts criticized Andrei Kozyrev and Boris Yeltsin for focusing excessively on the outside world. Today, many of Russia's leading statesmen can justly be criticized for focusing excessively on their new neighbors. Precisely because these new neighbors can no longer be seen as a unified or potentially unifiable community, Russian policy must strike an appropriate balance between the near- and far-abroads.

CONCLUSION

A revolution in the pattern of international relations is underway among Russia's new neighbors in Eurasia. It begins with the contraction and transformation of Russian power. The push from Moscow will no longer be Eurasia's defining force. Russia will not be able to create and sustain an unconquerable fortress on the territory of the former USSR that successfully protects it from the outside world.

Along the rim of Eurasia, China is emerging as a great, even a global, power. The other states of the rim are as free of interference from outside land or sea powers as they have been in several centuries.[20]

The relatively strong and stable among these states will moderate the trends toward Russian decline and will provide new energy from the outside. The failed states, stunted by their internal weakness or constrained by Russia's remaining leverage, will make this encounter between the center and the rimlands all the more dangerous and unpredictable.

The real question for Russian foreign policy toward its nearest neighbors cannot be simply how well integration is progressing. The kind of integration Russian policy makers have embraced as their ultimate goal is beyond the means of Russia and the desires of the new states themselves. Today, the most powerful impulses for integration outside Russia come from either the weakest of the CIS states or from states that need Russia to counter a present or potential regional threat. This group of states—a group as diverse as Tajikistan, Armenia, and Belarus—cannot truly become a Russian-led community that satisfies Russia's own needs. These states do not share any common perspective when they look at the opportunities and dangers of the new world. Only Russia sees the existing and potential challenges that surround it as a unified whole.[21] In such a setting, it is hard to imagine how Russia could become anything other than Gulliver perpetually constrained by Lilliputians.

The real question is whether Russia understands the broad strategic changes in Eurasia, adjusts to them, and adopts a policy that will diminish both the near-term threats from instability among its new neighbors and the long-term threats from the potential friction between Russia and the outside world on the territory of the former USSR. Russia need not abandon attempts to build normal, productive, and even integrated ties with its neighbors, but this integration will be more modest both in geography and scope than Moscow's current policies anticipate. In fact, a successful Russian strategy in its neighborhood has to be built upon cooperation with the most successful of the new states—an approach quite different from the Russian-dominated integrated community that still claims the allegiance of so many in Moscow. Russia must come to see the success and stability of Kazakhstan, Uzbekistan, and Ukraine as an essential element of this policy, and it should welcome the opportunity to share the burdens of maintaining stability in the former USSR with the most capable among its new neighbors.

To achieve this stability and to enhance its power and influence over ongoing changes, Russia must abandon—or at least radically modify—its goal of a tightly integrated CIS. It must also shift fundamentally its policies on CIS and bilateral mechanisms, making them both more responsive to the non-Russian states and more permeable to the outside world. Real progress is more likely to come through bilateral and multilateral agreements that include states outside the CIS than through CIS-only accords. These agreements will themselves be part of the breakdown of the post-Soviet space. The first seven years of Russian foreign policy have focused largely on opposing this breakdown. It is now time to recognize that this breakdown is inevitable and to work for changes that will lead to a region of stable and prosperous states—not one of weak states preyed upon by stronger neighbors. For such a possibility to emerge, much depends on Russia understanding its own interests and using its powers to break with a czarist and communist legacy—a legacy that is unsuited to the new world that has appeared and to the forces that will continue to shape Eurasia in the years ahead.

NOTES

[1] A. A. Kokoshin, *Armiya i politika: Sovietskaya voyenno-politicheskaya i voyenno-strategicheskaya mysl, 1918–1991 gody* (Moscow: Mezhdunarodnye Otnoshenia, 1995), p. 251.

[2] Yevgeny Primakov in *Trud*, June 25, 1996, and in *Krasnaya zvezda*, April 2, 1996. A similar argument was made by President Yeltsin in a June 1996 statement to the Federation Council on national security. It is even more evident in the draft of this document attributed to Yury Baturin and his staff that was published in a special section of *Nezavisimaya gazeta*, May 23, 1996, *NG-Stsenarii*, no. 2, May 1996, pp. 1–3. The president's finished report was published as "Poslanie Prezidenta Rossiiskoi Federatsii Federal'nomu Sobraniiu o natsional'noi bezopasnosti," *Nezavisimaya gazeta*, June 14, 1996.

[3] Sergei Kortunov, "Rossiya ishchet soyuznikov," *Nezavisimaya gazeta*, February 16, 1996, p. 4.

[4] On the diversity of views and problems that lurk behind the Russian foreign policy consensus on integration, see Sherman W.

Garnett, "The Integrationist Temptation," *Washington Quarterly*, vol. 18, no. 2 (Spring 1995), pp. 35–44.

5 See President Yeltsin's interview in *Segodnya*, July 1, 1996, p. 1.

6 Yeltsin's decree was published in *Rossiyskaya gazeta*, September 23, 1995, p. 4; a translation appeared in Foreign Broadcast Information Service, *FBIS Daily Report: Central Eurasia*, September 28, 1995.

7 Primakov in *Trud*, June 25, 1996, and *Krasnaya zvezda*, April 2, 1996.

8 *NG-Stsenarii*, p. 2.

9 "Address by President Boris Yeltsin to the Federal Assembly on the State of the Federation," *Federal News Service Transcripts*, February 23, 1996.

10 On the Foreign Policy Council, see the interview with Dmitriy Rurikov in *Interfax*, January 3, 1996; on the return of coordinating functions to the Ministry of Foreign Affairs, see the text of the decree in *Rossiiskaya gazeta*, March 16, 1996. The text of the Security Council decree was published in *Rossiiskaya gazeta*, July 16, 1996, p. 4; the announcement of the new Defense Council and its composition was in *ITAR-TASS*, July 25, 1996.

11 Igor Khripunov and Mary M. Matthews, "Russia's Oil and Gas Interest Group and Its Foreign Policy Agenda," *Problems of Post-Communism*, May/June 1996, pp. 38–48; Peter Rutland, "Russia's Energy Empire Under Strain," *Transition*, May 3, 1996, pp. 6–11; Rosemarie Forsythe, *The Politics of Oil in the Caucasus and Central Asia* (Oxford: International Institute for Strategic Studies and Oxford University Press, 1996).

12 These and other figures in this section are taken from the Economist Intelligence Unit's *Report on the Ukrainian Economy*, May 6, 1996, and a March 1996 report of the Kiev office of the World Bank, "On the Pillars of Economic Reform in Ukraine."

13 Authors' interviews with senior Russian defense officials and analysts.

14 *ITAR-TASS*, October 25, 1996.

15 *ITAR-TASS*, February 29, 1996.

16 "Speech by the President of Belarus Alexander Lukashenka at the State Duma Session (November 13, 1996)," *Federal News Service Transcripts*, November 13, 1996.

17 Vladimir Razuvayev, "Na poroge peremen," *Segodnya*, October 25, 1996, p. 9.

18 On developments in Russo-Chinese relations, see two recent reports by the authors of this chapter: Sherman W. Garnett, *Limited*

Partnership: Russia-China Relations in a Changing Asia (Washington: Carnegie Endowment for International Peace, 1998) and Dmitri Trenin, *Russia's China Problem* (Moscow: Carnegie Moscow Center, 1999).

[19] Alexei Salmin, "Opyt i perspektivy Sodruzhestva Nezavisimykh Gosudarstv," *Nezavisimaya gazeta*, May 15, 1996, p. 5.

[20] For an overview of the changes in Eurasia and Russia's problems in responding to them, see Sherman W. Garnett, "Russia's Illusory Ambitions," *Foreign Affairs*, vol. 76, no. 2 (March–April 1997), pp. 61–76.

[21] Dmitri Trenin, "Ot tashkentskogo dogovora k novomu varshavskomu?" *Segodnya*, December 2, 1995, p. 6.

About the Editors and Authors

Anders Åslund is a senior associate at the Carnegie Endowment for International Peace. He is the author of numerous books and articles on the post-Soviet economic transition, including *How Russia Became a Market Economy* (Brookings Institution, 1995).

Martha Brill Olcott is a senior associate at the Carnegie Endowment for International Peace and a professor of political science at Colgate University. She has written numerous studies on Central Asia and the Caucasus and on ethnic relations in the post-Soviet states, including *Kazakhstan: A Faint-Hearted Democracy* (Carnegie Endowment, forthcoming).

Mikhail Dmitriev is a scholar-in-residence at the Carnegie Moscow Center, where he codirects the Project on Post-Soviet Economies in Transition. In addition to conducting research and writing he has served in the Russian government, most recently as first deputy minister of labor.

Sherman W. Garnett, senior associate at the Carnegie Endowment for International Peace, is a specialist on the foreign and security policies of Russia and Ukraine. He is the author of *Keystone in the Arch: Ukraine in the Emerging Security Environment of Central and Eastern Europe* (Carnegie Endowment, 1997) and editor of forthcoming books on Russian–Chinese relations and on Belarus.

Michael McFaul is a senior associate at the Carnegie Endowment for International Peace and an assistant professor of political science at Stanford University, where he specializes in Russian domestic politics and elections. His most recent book is *Russia's 1996 Presidential Election: The End of Polarized Politics* (Hoover Institution Press, 1997).

Nikolai Petrov is a program associate at the Carnegie Moscow Center, where he specializes in social and political geography, regional development, ethnic-territorial claims and conflicts, and electoral studies. He also founded an independent policy research center in Russia and has served as an advisor to the Russian government.

Lilia Shevtsova is a senior associate at the Carnegie Endowment for International Peace, dividing her time between the Endowment's Washington offices and the Carnegie Moscow Center. She is one of Russia's best known and most respected political analysts and commentators. Her latest book is *Yeltsin's Russia: Myths and Reality* (Carnegie Endowment, 1999).

Valery Tishkov is a scholar-in-residence at the Carnegie Moscow Center and director of the Institute of Ethnology and Anthropology at the Russian Academy of Sciences. He is an expert on ethic issues and has served as chairman of the State Committee for Nationalities Affairs of the Russian Federation. His numerous books and articles on ethic minorities in the former Soviet Union include *Ethnicity, Nationalism, and Conflicts In and After the Soviet Union: The Mind Aflame* (London: Sage Publications, 1997).

Dimitri Trenin is the deputy director of the Carnegie Moscow Center and a senior research fellow at the Institute of Europe. A former Russian Army officer, he is a specialist in security and defense issues. The Carnegie Moscow Center published his study, *Kitaiskaya problema Rossii* (Russia's China problem), in 1998.

About the Carnegie Endowment

The Carnegie Endowment for International Peace was established in 1910 in Washington, D.C., with a gift from Andrew Carnegie. As a tax-exempt 501(c)(3) nonprofit organization, the Endowment conducts programs of research, discussion, publication, and education in international affairs and U.S. foreign policy. The Endowment publishes the quarterly magazine, *Foreign Policy*.

Carnegie's senior associates—whose backgrounds include government, journalism, law, academia, and public affairs—bring to their work substantial first-hand experience in foreign policy. Through writing, public and media appearances, study groups, and conferences, Carnegie associates seek to invigorate and extend both expert and public discussion on a wide range of international issues, including worldwide migration, nuclear non-proliferation, regional conflicts, multilateralism, democracy building, and the use of force. The Endowment also engages in and encourages projects designed to foster innovative contributions in international affairs.

In 1993, the Carnegie Endowment committed its resources to the establishment of a public policy research center in Moscow designed to promote intellectual collaboration among scholars and specialists in the United States, Russia, and other post-Soviet states. Together with the Endowment's associates in Washington, the center's staff of Russian and American specialists conduct programs on a broad range of major policy issues ranging from economic reform to civil-military relations. The Carnegie Moscow Center holds seminars, workshops, and study groups at which international participants from academia, government, journalism, the private sector, and nongovernmental institutions gather to exchange views. It also provides a forum for prominent international figures to present their views to informed Moscow audiences. Associates of the center also host seminars in Kiev, Ukraine, on an equally broad set of topics.

The Endowment normally does not take institutional positions on public policy issues. It supports its activities principally from its own resources, supplemented by nongovernmental, philanthropic grants.

Carnegie Endowment
for International Peace
1779 Massachusetts Ave., N.W.
Washington, D.C. 20036
Tel: 202-483-7600
Fax: 202-483-1840
E-mail: carnegie@ceip.org
Web: www.ceip.org

Carnegie Moscow Center
Ul. Tverskaya 16/2
7th Floor
Moscow 103009
Tel: 7-095-935-8904
Fax: 7-095-935-8906
E-mail: info@carnegie.ru
Web: www.carnegie.ru